A PORTRAIT OF
ITALY

Dwight V. Gast

TODTRI

This book was designed and produced by
TODTRI Book Publishers
254 West 31st Street
New York, NY 10001-2813
Fax: (212) 695-6984
E-mail: info@todtri.com

Visit us on the web!
www.todtri.com

Printed and bound in Korea

ISBN 1-57717-090-3

Author: Dwight Gast

Publisher: Robert M. Tod
Editors: Mary Forsell, Joanna Wissinger, Don Kennision
Designer: Mark Weinberg
Production Co-ordinator: Heather Weigel
DTP Associate: Adam Yellin
Typesetting: Command-O Design

PHOTO CREDITS

Photographer/Page Number

G. Barone/FPG International 51
Dave Bartruff 142, 143 (top & bottom)
Randa Bishop 16, 68
Charles Bowman/Picture Perfect USA 5, 7, 24-25, 71, 96, 97, 112 (bottom), 113, 114-115, 116, 117,
   118, 120-121, 123, 129, 130
Jean S. Buldain/Picture Perfect USA 81 (bottom)
Bullaty Lomeo 8-9, 20, 28 (top & bottom), 29, 30 (left), 30-31, 32 (top), 42 (bottom), 48-49,
   49 (top & bottom), 58 (bottom) 60, 61, 78 (bottom), 84 (top), 86, 88-89, 90, 91 (top & bottom),
   92, 99, 100, 102 (bottom), 106 (left), 110, 133 (top), 135-136, 139 (bottom)
Sonja Bullaty 22 (top), 26, 27, 46-47, 55, 58 (top), 77, 78 (top), 95, 98, 101 (bottom), 112 (top), 126
Hanya Chlala/Picture Perfect USA 21
Stephanie Colasanti/Picture Perfect USA 39, 52 (top & bottom), 53, 83 (bottom)
Michael DeFreitas 103 (top)
James John Doro/Picture Perfect USA 127
Ric Ergenbright 32 (bottom), 33, 45, 64 (bottom), 134, 135, 139 (top), 140 (top & bottom)
Robert Fried 80, 81 (top), 108, 109
Stephen Graham/Dembinsky Photo Associates 11, 70 (bottom), 104-105, 133 (bottom)
Bill Holden/Picture Perfect USA 40-41, 44 (bottom), 59, 65, 101 (top), 122, 138 (top & bottom)
Dave & Les Jacobs/Picture Perfect USA 13, 14, 15, 18, 19, 22 (bottom)
Doranne Jacobson 17 (top & bottom), 69 (top & bottom), 102 (top), 106 (right), 111
Ken Laffal 54, 63, 64 (top), 66 (top & bottom), 67, 70 (top), 72-73, 74, 75, 76, 82, 83 (top), 84 (bottom)
Graham Lawrence/Picture Perfect USA 44 (top)
Angelo Lomeo 6, 56-57, 78-79, 93, 94
Joachim Messerschmidt/FPG International 50
John Miller/Picture Perfect USA 12, 42 (top)
Hugh Rooney/Picture Perfect USA 23, 103 (bottom), 107, 119, 132
Vadim Sokolov/Picture Perfect USA 34, 35 (top & bottom), 36 (top & bottom), 37, 38, 128, 131
Charlie Waite/Picture Perfect USA 43, 62, 85, 87, 124, 125, 141

TABLE OF CONTENTS

Dramatic statuary in silhouette at St Peter's.

Introduction

*I*taly has something for practically everyone—and no wonder. The country's twenty regions, finally brought together under one central government in 1870, remain delightfully distinct. From sultry Sicilians to shrewd Venetians—and everything in between—the many facets of the Italian character reflect a country that is a true gem. What really unifies Italy is its beauty: 'Oh, Italia', wrote Lord Byron, 'thou hast the fatal gift of beauty.... The orphans of the heart must turn to thee'. Other orphans of the heart included Johann Wolfgang von Goethe, Percy Bysshe Shelley, Stendhal, Geoffrey Chaucer, and John Milton, as well as two who remained forever: Elizabeth Barrett Browning, who is buried in the English cemetery in Florence, and John Keats, who wrote the epitaph on his simple tomb in Rome, 'Here lies one whose name was writ in water'.

Italy's regional diversity is due in part to the varied peoples who settled the country. By the year 2000 BC, Italic tribes had established themselves on the peninsula. Around 1200 BC, the mysterious Etruscans began making an appearance in central Italy. They were followed by the Greeks, who established colonies collectively known as Magna Graecia in southern Italy, largely in present-day Apulia. Rivalling Greek control was Carthage, the Phoenician colony in northern Africa that was allied with the Etruscans. Over the centuries, Greeks and Carthaginians fought it out in Sicily and, to some extent, Sardinia.

It is, however, the ancient Romans whom we most closely associate with Italy. According to a legend made famous by the Roman historian Livy and the poet Virgil, Rome was founded on April 21 in the year 753 BC by Romulus and Remus, the twin sons of the vestal virgin Rhea Silvia, who had been raped by Mars, the war god. Fearing rivalry for the throne, the treacherous King Amulius set the boys adrift on the river Tiber. They were cast ashore near the desolate Palatine hill, where they were nursed by a she-wolf 'who heard their wails and very tenderly gave them her teats".

Romulus's rule was followed by that of three Sabine kings and three Etruscan kings. In 509 BC, the city state's great landowners ended the first monarchy and founded the Roman Republic. Over the next few centuries Rome gradually extended its boundaries throughout the peninsula. With the defeat of the Greek colony of Tarentum (modern-day Taranto) in 272 BC and the Etruscan city of Volsinii (Orvieto) in 265 BC, the Romans gained control of mainland Italy, to which it added Spain, Greece, and eventually Gaul.

This period also saw a great deal of strife between the founding patricians and the plebeians, culminating in the first century BC with civil wars and the rise of Julius Caesar as dictator. Assassinated in 44 BC, Julius Caesar's rule soon gave way, in 27 BC, to an imperial monarchy under his nephew, Augustus. During Augustus's reign Egypt was added to the Roman Empire, which stretched from the Rhine and the Danube in the west to the Syrian desert in the east. Beginning with Claudius in AD 43, Britain was added to the roster.

A Ligurian farm.

In the second century, there were periods of peace under such emperors as Trajan, Hadrian, and Marcus Aurelius, to be shattered on the death of Commodus in the year 198. In 284, Diocletian restored order and divided the administration of the empire among five leaders. His successor as emperor, Constantine, moved the capital to Constantinople, opening the way in Italy for barbarian invaders from the north. By 476 the last Roman emperor, Romulus Augustus, was dethroned by Odoacer, a barbarian general. From 488 to 526, Theodoric, king of the Ostrogoths, ruled Italy from Ravenna, where he built dazzling churches that are still standing today. The Byzantine emperor Justinian subsequently defeated the Goths even as the Lombards established their own dynasty. In 754, Pope Stephen II called on Pepin, king of

the Franks, to expel the Lombards from Rome. In 800, Pope Leo III crowned another Frank king, Charlemagne, as the first emperor of the Holy Roman Empire. The coronation took place on a porphyry slab that even today sits in front of the central door of St Peter's in Rome. The authority of the Holy Roman Empire, however, was often largely nominal even in the north, while the south was invaded by Saracens and Normans.

Beginning in the eleventh century, democratically governed city-states began to take shape in the northern cities of the Veneto, Lombardy, Umbria, and Tuscany as the south became feudal under the Norman king Roger II—a system that endured well into the twentieth century. In 1154, Frederick Barbarossa, leading a force of three thousand men, attempted unsuccessfully to unite Italy. Around the same time, most of the Italian city-states were forced to choose sides, becoming either supporters of the pope (Guelphs) or of the emperor (Ghibellines). The city-states prospered, even though democratic rule had given way to government by powerful local families: the Visconti and the Sforza in Milan; the Gonzaga in Mantua, the Malatesta in Rimini, the Este in Ferrara, and the Medici in Florence. Preeminent among them were the Medici, who established Florence's power and prestige once and for all until the death of Lorenzo the Magnificent in 1492.

What followed was a series of foreign dominations, from the French takeover of Milan and Naples to their routing by Charles V, the Hapsburg king of Spain who became Holy

A panoramic view of Florence along the Arno River. Of note, from left to right, are the tower of the Palazzo Vecchio, the dome of the church of San Lorenzo, the bell tower of the cathedral of Santa Maria del Fiore, and the cathedral dome.

Roman Emperor. Eventually the Spanish Hapsburgs dominated Italy, with the exception of Venice and the duchy of Savoy-Piedmont, until the War of The Spanish Succession left Italy largely in the hands of the Austrians. By 1806, Napoleon had annexed large portions of Italy, including Rome, Piedmont, and Venetian possessions in Dalmatia, while he abandoned the twelve-hundred-year-old Venetian Republic to Austria. Largely under the guidance of Giuseppe Mazzini, a republican idealogue from Genoa, this was followed in subsequent years by liberal revolts in Naples, Turin, Milan, Rome, and Palermo. Piedmont, with its liberal constitution and military might, emerged as the only political entity capable of providing concrete leadership for the Risorgimento, as the movement for Italian unity was called. Count Camillo Cavour, prime minister of Piedmont, began annexations of Italy. Freedom fighter Giuseppe Garibaldi added Naples and Sicily to the newly united Italy, and a third war with Austria resulted in the inclusion of the Veneto in 1866. In 1870, with the entry of General Cadorna into Rome, unification was complete.

Over the next few decades, Italy was ruled as a constitutional monarchy, dominated by politicians from Piedmont. In an effort to take its place on the international front, Italy sent troops to Africa to seize parts of Eritrea and Somalia and make an unsuccessful bid for Ethiopia. Instead, it won possession of Libya and the Dodecanese Islands. After much debate, Italy entered World War I on the side of France and Britain with the promise of the return of Trentino, Trieste, Istria, and Alto Adige, as well as other parcels of land, which were not given back to Italy. Morale was low—600,000 Italians were lost in the fighting—and the country became ripe for takeover by Fascist Benito Mussolini.

Though Mussolini did accomplish the signing in 1929 of a concordat with the Holy See ending the fifty-year breach between church and state, most of his other actions were not so productive, such as the occupation of Ethiopia and the unsuccessful campaigns in France, Greece, Africa, and the Soviet Union. Allied with Adolf Hitler's Germany and Japan, Mussolini was forced to resign upon the arrival of Allied forces in Sicily in 1943. Power was restored to King Victor Emmanuel III, Marshal Pietro Badoglio was appointed prime minister, an armistice was signed with the Allies, and war was declared on Germany.

In the south of the country, the Committee of National Liberation was established by some six anti-Fascist parties, while in the north resistance activities were carried out by several groups, particularly the Communists. Following the liberation of Rome in June 1944, a six-party government was set up by Ivanoe Bonomi. The following year, Mussolini was killed by partisans as he tried to flee to Switzerland.

The end of World War II brought about the reshaping of Italy. Istria, Zara, and Adriatic islands were given back to Yugoslavia, and Italy also had to relinquish claims on its African colonies and the Dodecanese Islands. Trieste, Alto Adige, and the Valle d'Aosta were definitively given to Italy, however. The monarchy once again abolished, elections were held in 1946 to establish a new constitution, which was written and approved the following year. In 1948 the first national elections were held under the new constitution, giving the Christian Democrat (Democrazia Cristiana, or DC) party a majority, which it has held ever since. Second in popularity until recently was the Communist party, now known as the Partito Democratico Sinistra, or PDS. Another party with a sizeable membership is the Socialist party (Partito Socialista Italiano, or PSI). But there are many parties in Italian politics, with new ones gaining strength all the time. Such political and historical diversity have given Italy its wide-ranging makeup, and to visit there is not to experience one country but many.

*The vast interior of St Peter's was worked on by a number of artists.
Here, Bernini's baldacchino, an ornamental structure over the main
altar that is the culmination of all his work in the great basilica.*

Northern Italy

Well before the advent of the cruise ship and the airplane, northern Italy was most visitors' point of entry to the country. To many, in fact, it was a final destination. On Lake Como alone lived William Wordsworth; Shelley and Byron visited; and D. H. Lawrence made his home here. They were attracted by the unexpectedly lush scenery of the Lake Country, which is but one aspect of northern Italy's beauty. The architectural fairyland of Venice, the stately Palladian villas of the Veneto, the Dolomites of Trentino/Alto Adige, the art and architecture of Milan, the smaller cities of Lombardy, the baroque splendours of Turin, the natural wonders of the Parco Nazionale del Gran Paradiso in the Valle d'Aosta, the historical and present-day charms of Liguria—all combine to richly reward the visitor to this part of Italy.

Northern Italy also boasts a variety of unique cuisines, influenced in part by its German- and French-speaking neighbours. It is the best place to try risotto, the soupy rice staple that is more popular than pasta, along with polenta, a cornmeal mush that is eaten as a first course. Many of the area's wines are already widely known from export: Barolo, Bardolino, Valpolicella, Soave, Spumante. Others, including grappa, await the visitor in situ.

Venice

O happy streets! to rumbling wheels unknown,
No carts, no coaches shake the floating town!

What John Gay wrote about Venice in Trivia in 1716 is still true today. Perhaps the motoscafi and other motor craft occasionally 'shake the floating town', but by and large Venice has remained free of

Sunset over the Venetian lagoon.

Sala Comacina on Lake Como is just one example of the delightful towns that abound in the lake country.

the hustle and bustle of the rest of the civilised world. The first thing one notices is the absence of automobiles, which even as the streets are replaced by water are themselves replaced by boats. There are numerous occasions to see every kind of boat imaginable if the visitor comes at special times of year. The Vogalonga, which takes place on the Sunday after Ascension Day, is a 32-kilometre (51-mile) race open to any type of boat and any number of oarsmen. For the Festa del Redentore, which takes place the third Sunday in July, a bridge of boats is constructed across the Giudecca Canal, just as it is across the Grand Canal for the Festa della Salute November 21. The Regata Storica, held the first Sunday in September, consists of various processions and boat races.

At all times of the year, however, Venice diplays its glories. In the warmer months it attracts crowds to the extent that Henry James felt compelled to write, 'The Venice of today is a vast museum where the little wicket that admits you is perpetually turning and creaking, and you march through the institution with a herd of fellow-gazers'. In the cooler months Venice truly earns its sobriquet, La Serenissma, meaning the Most Serene Republic, unless of course it is carnival time, when thousands of people from all over the world dress in fanciful, outlandish costumes and celebrate the pre-Lenten holidays.

A visit to Venice begins with Piazza San Marco, which despite its attraction to tourists is still the centre of Venetian life. Called by Napoleon 'the finest drawing room in Europe', the piazza is enclosed on three sides by the repetitive facades of two handsome public buildings, called the procuratie, and the Ala Napoleonica, or Napoleonic Wing, an addition that houses the Museo Correr, a collection of paintings related to Venice. Also housed in the procuratie are shops and cafes, including Caffe Florian, the oldest in Venice and still fitted out with its original eighteenth-century furnishings.

A bell tower presides over this view of Venice's St Mark's square. Prominent are the Libreria Sansoviana, begun by Sansovino in 1537, and the Doges' Palace, the former official residence of the doges.

A view of the rich spectacle of the Grand Canal as seen from the Accademia Bridge. In the distance is the grandiose church of Santa Maria della Salute, built over a fifty-year period (1631-81) by Baldassare Longheni in thanksgiving for deliverance of Venice from the plague.

This sculpture from the tomb of a Venetian knight depicts its subject as sleeping, his hands clasped in a gesture of piety.

The inside of St Mark's basilica is covered with gold mosaics depicting everything from scenes from the Old Testament and the Life of Christ to the transportation of the body of St Mark from Alexandria to Venice.

Gondoliers plying their trade in a canal before the ancient palazzi of Venice.

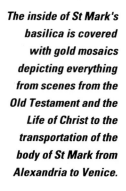

'Nothing is sweeter to the human eye than the sight of gold', wrote Lorenzo Da Ponte, the Venetian-born author of three librettos for Mozart, and these mosaics on the outside of Venice's St Mark's basilica are very sweet indeed.

The piazza takes its name from the Basilica di San Marco, rising at its end of the piazza like a 'a vast warty bug taking a meditative walk', as Mark Twain was wont to describe it. According to legend, in the year 828 two Venetian merchants doing business in Moslem Alexandria took the body of St Mark, safely concealed beneath a mass of salted pork. The scene is vividly depicted in a mosaic on the right pillar next to the main altar, in which a tiny boat bearing the body of the saint navigates against a huge sky of gold. The caption reads 'kefir, kefir vociferantur', ('pork, pork they shout'). Over this relic the church grew in various stages, resulting in the magnificent mix of Byzantine, Romanesque, and Gothic styles of today. Strangely, it was only designated the cathedral of Venice in 1807, replacing San Pietro di Castello. Most of the countless capitals, statues, bas-reliefs, and columns adorning the basilica inside and out were brought back as booty from the East.

One could spend days looking at the cathedral, beginning with the four horses on the facade (they are copies—the originals are in the adjacent museum) brought from Constantinople after the Fourth Crusade. Other noteworthy features are the marble floor, the wall-to-wall mosaics dating from the eleventh to the sixteenth centuries, and the immense gold-plated and jewel-encrusted altarpiece called the Pala d'Oro.

Next to the basilica is the Palazzo Ducale, or Doges' Palace, the former official residence of the doge, where the patrician parliament and government offices were housed as well. A triumph of Gothic engineering, the open space on the façade of the Palazzo Ducale gives it (as it does with many a Venetian palazzo) a sense of

Designed by Palladio, Venice's San Giorgio Maggiore is still used for worship. It represents one of the architect's greatest achievements, an application of his principles concerning the relationship between architecture and environment and a façade derived from his study of Roman antiquity.

*Carnival revellers in
their brilliantly coloured
costumes in Venice.
A mainstay of Venetian
life in the eighteenth
century, Carnival was
reinstituted a few
years ago to give
winter tourism a boost.*

lightness, further emphasised by the water. Inside, the most impressive feature is the Sala del Maggior Consiglio, built in 1340 as the largest hall in Europe without inside support. This is where the Maggior Consiglio, a patrician ruling body consisting of three to four percent of the population, met and elected the doge for life, as well as determined the more limited terms of his counselors, the senate, judges, and all other magistrates.

An entire wall of the Sala del Maggior Consiglio is occupied by Jacopo Tintoretto's Paradise (the largest painting ever made), and one of the ovals on the ceiling contains Paolo Veronese's The Apotheosis of Venice. A 1600 addition to the Palazzo Ducale is the Ponte dei Sospiri, or Bridge of Sighs, so called because through it passed prisoners from the prisons to be examined by the state inquisitors.

Back outside in the Piazza San Marco is the clock tower called the Torre dell'Orologio, designed by Mauro Codussi in 1496, on which the hours are struck by two large bronze Moors. Across the piazza looms the Campanile of San Marco, which was begun in 888 and collapsed in 1902, destroying it as well as the loggetta by Sansovino at its base. Both structures were carefully, almost immediately restored. Nearby is the Piazzetta, where two huge columns display more booty, namely a winged lion fashioned from a chimera and a statue of St Theodore, the original patron saint of Venice. Opposite the Palazzo Ducale is the Libreria Marciana, designed by Sansovino based on classical prototypes. Sansovino was also responsible for the Zecca, the Doric building around the corner.

A number of other noteworthy sights lie within walking distance of Piazza San Marco. The Riva degli Schiavoni leads to the Giardini Pubblici, a lovely park where, on odd years, the Biennale d'Arte, a much-vaunted international art exhibition, is held. For colour of a more local variety, there is the Mercerie, the city's main shopping street. This leads to the Rialto Bridge, and on the other side are outdoor produce and fish markets.

*Venice's Piazza San Marco
as seen from its bell tower.
Napoleon called the square
'the finest drawing room in
Europe'; today it draws crowds
to its cafes, an important part
of everyday life in Venice.*

Windows on a Venetian Gothic palazzo. Venice produced its own version of Gothic architecture, heavily influenced by the Byzantine and other exotic cultures with which Venice had commercial or political ties.

An array of lively Baroque statuary amidst the volutes on the church of Santa Maria della Salute in Venice.

Gondolas on the waterfront at twilight are a romantic sight in this most romantic of cities, Venice.

A sculptural detail enhances the architecture of a Palladian villa.

A view of the Teatro Olimpico, Palladio's last work, in Vicenza. Following the creation of his familiar Vitruvius, the architect tried to make Olimpico into a classical space, but opted to modernise it instead to meet the architectural and theatrical standards of his time.

The city of Vicenza is virtually a homage to Andrea Palladio, the sixteenth-century architect who moved to the city from his native Padua in his early childhood and built some of his best palazzi here, as well as many villas in the surounding countryside.

The Veneto

Of the cities in the Veneto, Treviso is nearest to Venice. Its peaceful setting on the gentle Sile River belies the fact that such textile giants as Benetton and Stefanel are located here. But for the visitor, it is the past that matters, and a stroll through Treviso's Città Vecchia (Old City), taking in the Romanesque Palazzo dei Trecento and the Palazzo del Podestà, as well as the transitional Gothic church of San Nicolò and the Renaissance Duomo, is as relaxing as it is charming.

More bustle is to be found in Padua, which boasts a still-functioning university founded in 1222. Here is where Dante, Francesco Petrarch, and Torquato Tasso studied and Galileo taught. The city's religious monuments are its main attractions, however, and include the Cappella degli Scrovegni (decorated with extraordinary frescoes by Giotto in the fourteenth century) and the Basilica of Il Santo, where Donatello's equestrian monument stands proudly on the square and other treasures by the Renaissance sculptor are housed.

Vicenza is a virtual tribute to Andrea Palladio, who moved there from his native Padua during his early childhood. His local masterworks include a number of palazzi, as well as the Piazza dei Signori and, most famously, the Teatro Olimpico, his last work, based on the principles of Vitruvius. Near Vicenza proper are other artistic marvels. The Basilica of Monte Berico contains a huge canvas by Veronese; the Villa Valmarana houses frescoes by Giovanni Battista Tiepolo and his son, Giandomenico.

Verona is a cornucopia of architecture, from its ancient Roman Arena, still filled each summer night by crowds of some twenty thousand during opera season, to the medieval Piazza della Erbe and Piazza dei Signori, to the Romanesque church of San Zeno Maggiore, where a lovely triptych by Mantegna can be viewed. The legacy of the Della Scala family, who once ruled Verona, is the Arche Scaligere. Possibly more fictitious are the sites associated with Juliet Capulet—a tomb, house, and balcony. Take it all in from the vantage point of the terraced garden of Palazzo Giusti.

The most singularly spectacular part of the Veneto, at least as far as nature is concerned, are the Dolomites. Rising straight up to more than 3,030 metres (10,000 feet), these pinkish stone pinnacles were once coral reefs. It is here that the village of Cortina d'Ampezzo, a chic ski resort, is found. Other pleasant venues range from the village of Pieve di Cadore, with its museum of memorabilia to Titian, and Belluno, which is distinguished by its sixteenth-century cathedral.

*A full house at Verona's Roman Arena
watches a production of Verdi's Aida, one
of the mainstays of the summer opera season.*

*The ancient amphitheatre of Verona, the Roman Arena is virtually
undamaged despite being two thousand years old. It fills with a crowd
of twenty thousand spectators every evening during summer opera season.*

Monte Cervino, in English known as the Matterhorn, is here reflected in all its glory in a cool alpine lake, Lago Blu.

Crisp whitewashed houses stand out against the green grass of this alpine village.

Trentino/Alto Adige

In 1918 the regions of Italian-speaking Trentino and German-speaking Alto Adige were annexed to Italy from Austria. Cultural links between Alto Adige and neighbouring Austria remain strong, however, despite the autonomy given the region by the Italian government. Today, while the Trentino remains Italian-speaking, only some thirty-five percent of the total population of Alto Adige speak Italian as their first language; the remainder speak German as well as isolated pockets of Ladin. For the visitor, the net result is a fascinating blend of influences unlike anywhere else in Italy.

Trento, the largest city in the Trentino, is best remembered as the site of the Council of Trent, a meeting of Catholic bishops held between 1545 and 1563 as a response to the Reformation taking place elsewhere in Europe. Many of the palazzi where the Catholic prelates lived during the council still stand along stately Via Belenzani. These palazzi—along with the Romanesque cathedral, the eleventh-century Torre Civico, the thirteenth-century Castelletto dei Vescovi, and the thirteenth-century Castello del Buonconsiglio—comprise the principal man-made sights in the spectacular mountain setting of the city.

The mountains, dotted with castles and small villages, have made Trentino an important destination for tourists. The most famous ski resort in the region is the town of Madonna di Campiglio; others include the village of Pinzolo, which boasts fascinating frescoes at its church of San Vigilio, as well as Cavalese.

The Alto Adige (it takes its name from the river Adige, the longest in Italy after the Po) offers a similar blend of natural and man-made charms. The Val Venosta contains such wonders as the Abbey of Monte Maria, the Castello di Coira, and the Schloss Kastelbell. Cities include the health spa Merano, with its Gothic Castello Principesco and cathedral, and the nearby twelfth-century Castel Tirolo.

Medieval Bolzano features a Gothic cathedral, the Convento dei Domenicani, the church of the Francescani (which houses an impressive altarpiece of the Cappella della Vergine), and the Castel Roncolo, with its secular Gothic frescoes depicting knights and damsels from popular tales of chivalry. Another pleasant town is Bressanone, which boasts a lovely cathedral dating from the thirteenth century as well as a seventeenth-century Palazzo dei Principi Vescovi, where the Tirol bishops once resided.

Lombardy/The Lakes

Industrious Milan, the second-largest city in Italy, is the country's main industrial centre as well as its most important railway junction and seat of Italy's banking and commerce. Though heavily bombed during World War II, there is much historic architecture in the midst of the modern construction. The cathedral, the world's largest after St Peter's in Rome, is the only truly Gothic building in Italy, though it is a highly idiosyncratic Gothic, studded with pinnacles and statues. Even earlier are the lovely Romanesque churches of Sant'Ambrogio, San Lorenzo, and San Nazaro Maggiore. Other important religious structures are Bramante's church of San Satiro, Santa Maria delle Grazie (the refectory of which houses Leonardo da Vinci's Last Supper), San Marco, San Simpliciano, Santa Maria della Passione, San Pietro in Gessate, Santa Maria Presso San Celso, and Sant'Eustorgio. Noteworthy secular structures include the Palazzo Reale, Filarete's Ospedale Maggiore, Teatro alla Scala, and the Castello Sforzesco. This latter structure, built by Francesco Sforza on the site of a fourteenth-century castle of the Visconti by a team of architects and designers (including Filarete, Bramante, and da Vinci), now houses a number of interesting museums. Their subjects are quite diverse, ranging from archaeological material of prehistoric Lombardy through the Rondanini Pietà (Michelangelo's last work) and works by Titian and Mantegna to eighteenth-century Lombard, Neapolitan, and Venetian art. The finest collection of northern Italian painting, however, is to be found at the Pinacoteca di Brera, which houses masterpieces from all over the region brought together under one roof by Napoleon. A little gem of a museum is the Museo Poldi-Pezzoli, formerly a private collection of everything from antique arms and armor to Antonio Pollaiolo's Portrait of a Lady, which has become something of a mascot of the museum. Another important Milanese art museum is the Pinacoteca Ambrosiana, where works by Leonardo da Vinci, Titian, Botticelli, and Raphael are kept.

Milan's Galleria Vittorio Emanuele II, designed in 1878 by Giuseppe Mengoni as a prototypical shopping mall so successfully as to earn it the epithet 'il Salotto di Milano' (the drawing room of Milan).

Inside Milan's Galleria Vittorio Emanuele II, where four iron and glass streets with neo-Renaissance facades converge on a central domed piazza. The galleria is filled with shops and restaurants.

The roof of Milan's cathedral, second in the world only to St Peter's in size. A visit here provides an opportunity to see close up the many statues of saints, sinners, knights, pilgrims, and fanciful gargoyles.

A madonnaro, or 'street artist', in Milan has made an elaborate pastel drawing for the delectation of passersby.

Pigeons and people animate this lively square in Milan.

Milan's cathedral and monument to Vittorio Emanuele II. The cathedral was begun in 1386 and brought to a hasty conclusion in 1813, though the bronze portals of its facade were completed in this century.

Other noteworthy venues in Milan include Italy's most important natural history museum, the Gallery of Modern Art, the Museo di Milano, the Museo di Storia Contemporanea, the Leonardo da Vinci Museum of Science and Technology, and the newly opened Civico Museo d'Arte Contemporanea.

Outside Milan are more Lombard treasures. The cathedral of Monza houses the Iron Crown of Lombardy. According to legend it was made from a nail from the true cross and was used for the coronation of everyone from Barbarossa to Napoleon. Also in Monza is the Villa Reale, which blooms with elaborate English gardens. Another fine cathedral—designed by Bramante and da Vinci, among others—is to be found in Pavia, which also boasts two noteworthy churches, San Michele and San Pietro in Ciel d'Oro, as well as an excellent museum in its Castello Visconteo. The town's main attraction, however, is the extraordinary Certosa, the most famous Carthusian charterhouse after the Grande Chartreuse near Grenoble. Also worth a visit, Cremona is home to the magnificent Piazza del Comune, in which stand a Romanesque cathedral and the tallest bell tower in Italy. Also found here are the excellent Museo Civico and the Museo Stradivariano, which displays material related to Antonio Stradivari, the violin maker.

Despite these worthwhile attractions, Lombardy's biggest draw are its lakes, and each has its own peculiar charms. Lago Maggiore, which is also bordered by the region of Piedmont (Lago d'Orta is entirely in Piedmont) and Switzerland, is dotted with the Borromean Islands and such picturesque villages as Stresa and Castiglione Olona, where there are frescoes by the fifteenth-century Florentine artist Masolino.

Lago Lugano, half of which is in Switzerland, is noteworthy for its stark mountain scenery. Lago di Como has long attracted English visitors such as Wordsworth, Byron, Shelley, and Lawrence. Towns on the lake include Como, which boasts a harmonious Gothic-Renaissance cathedral with paintings by Luini; Bellagio, a lovely Lombard town; and Lecco, where Alessandro Manzoni partly set his novel The Betrothed. Lago d'Iseo is a relatively quiet lake surrounded by quaint villages, olive groves, and spectacular mountain scenery. On Lago di Garda, the largest of the lakes, is the town of Sirmione, dominated by the thirteenth-century crenellated castle of the Scaligeri, lords of nearby Verona.

Sirmione, on Lago di Garda, has been a spa since ancient times. Wealthy Romans favored Sirmione as a summer residence, and the Roman poet Catullus, had a villa here.

Lazize, on the eastern shore of Lago di Garda, still retains part of its medieval wall. It has been succeeded by Bardolino as the chief port on its shore, but as these colourful boats attest is still popular with residents and visitors alike.

Once a fortified town and still retaining some interesting old houses, Garda is located on the shores of Lago di Garda. Famous under both Romans and Longobards, it had origins even more ancient, as testified by an early necropolis on the outskirts.

The Rocca Scaligera in Sirmione on Lago di Garda was a stronghold of the Scaliger family, lords of Verona. Dante Alighieri is said to have stayed there. Illumination accentuates its grandeur, especially the massive central tower.

Valle d'Aosta

The French-speaking region of the Valle d'Aosta has been autonomous since 1948. Such natural features as Mont Blanc, the Matterhorn, Monte Rosa, and Gran Paradiso combine with Roman ruins and medieval castles to create one of the most spectacular areas in Italy. Numerous summer and winter resorts are found there.

The region's capital city, Aosta, has been important since Roman times as the gateway to the Great and Little Saint Bernard passes through the Alps. It has preserved its Roman town walls and such other ancient monuments as the Arch of Augustus, as well as the church of Sant'Orso, with its eleventh-century frescoes and Renaissance cathedral.

In addition to such memorable sights as the medieval castle of Fenis and the magnificently situated village of Entreves, one of the most spectacular aspects of the Valle d'Aosta is the Gran Paradiso National Park. Originally established as a hunting preserve for King Victor Emmanuel II, the park is now a wildlife refuge that prohibits hunting and is the only part of the Alps where the ibex flourishes in its natural state, along with chamois and alpine marmot.

A small farm in the Valle d'Aosta exemplifies the importance of agriculture in the region.

43

Situated in a deep vale at the southern foot of the Mont Blanc range is Courmayeur, the so-called Chamonix of Piedmont. It is visited in summer by both alpinists and lovers of mountain scenery and is also a famous winter sports resort.

Skiing and winter sports of all kinds are popular pastimes for Italians, who boast some of the best slopes in the world.

Modern roads link once isolated villages in the Valle d'Aosta.

Piedmont

The westernmost region in Italy, Piedmont was once under Roman rule before being held by the Lombards and Franks and sacked by Magyars and Saracens. In the eleventh century it became part of the house of Savoy, and over the centuries was disputed by the Hapsburgs and France. With the unification of Italy, Turin, the capital of Piedmont, enjoyed a brief tenure as capital of Italy.

One of the first regions in the country to undergo industrialisation, today Piedmont is known as the manufacturing centre for Fiat and Pirelli, among others, but there is much of interest to the visitor as well.

Turin is a stately city laid out in a grid pattern dating from Roman times, although its real beauty lies in the works of architects Guarino Guarini and Filippo Juvara, who remade Turin in a somewhat restrained baroque style. Among its monuments are the Palazzo Madama (Juvara did its western front), which is a repository of antique art, and the Palazzo Reale, with its collection of arms and armor. Other monuments of note are the cathedral, in which Guarini's circular chapel houses the Shroud of Turin; Guarini's Palazzo Carignano, which contains the Museo Nazionale del Risorgimento Italiano, whose purpose is to trace Italy's struggle for unification; the Palazzo dell'Accademia delle Scienze, home of a renowned Egyptian Museum (Museo Egizio) and a picture gallery called the Galleria Sabauda; and the Palazzo di Citta.

Other museums are devoted to modern art and Oriental art. For an overview of Turin, go to the top of the Mole Antonelliana or to the hilltop Museo Nazionale della Montagna. Also on the outskirts are Juvara's Basilica di Superga (called the Savoy Pantheon, since many members of the illustrious House of Savoy are buried there) and the same architect's hunting lodge at Stupigni.

Row upon row of regularly planted trees lend beauty to Piedmont.

Grapes are ready for the harvest in Piedmont when they turn a robust red.

After being picked, the grapes are crushed.

Finally, the grapes' bounty is bottled and kept in the wine cellar.

Liguria

Stretched out along the Mediterranean between France and Tuscany like a boomerang, Liguria is a thin sliver of land, one of the smallest regions in Italy. But it is not short on things for the visitor to do. Its capital, Genoa, has the largest intact medieval quarter of any city in the world and many other monuments from its proud past. On either side of Genoa extend two rivieras. To the west lies the Riviera di Ponente, known for its flower-growing industry and increasingly for its resorts. To the east is the Riviera di Levante, where more resorts mingle with quiet fishing villages. It is all sheltered from the rest of the continent by mountains, which give it a mild climate year-round.

Much remains of Genoa's proud past to remind the visitor that the city has earned the epithet La Superba. Among the highlights are the Palazzo Ducale, the opera house Teatro Carlo Felice, the Cathedral, the Palazzo di San Giorgio, the church of Santa Maria di Carignano, the church of Santissima Annunziata, and the church of San Matteo, which contains many mementos of the Doria family; the square in front of the church contains several of the family's palazzi. On a less grand scale is the restored childhood home of Christopher Columbus. (Columbus is but one of Genoa's native sons—others include heroes Giuseppe Mazzini and Giuseppe Garibaldi, as well as violin virtuoso Niccolo Paganini.) Another site associated with Columbus is the church where he was baptised, Santo Stefano, clad in the black-and-white stone so typical of Genoa.

Many of Genoa's venerable buildings house wonderful art collections, among them Palazzo Bianco, Palazzo Rosso, Palazzo Reale, and Palazzo Spinola. Just outside of town is the Campo Santo or Cimitero di Staglieno, one of the most famous cemeteries in Italy, full of interesting nineteenth-century tomb sculpture.

The medieval cupola and the campanile of this church and its parish are just some of the many things which provide compelling evidence of the Middle Ages in Genoa.

Built by Giovanni Angelo Francone and Pier Franc in the middle of the 17th century, Genoa's Palazzo Reale was finished by Carlo Fontana in 1705. Today the building has become the center of a collection in its unique staterooms by such painters as van Dyck, who also has Crucified Christ *in the Saletta dei Fiamminghi.*

Rapallo, in a sheltered position at the head of its gulf, is the best-known holiday resort of the Riviera di Levante. Popular in both summer and winter, its lovely surroundings are the main attraction.

Portovenere, the ancient Portus Veneris, a dependency of Genoa since 1113, is a charming fortified village built on the sloping shore of the Bocchetta, a narrow strait separating the Isola Palmaria from the mainland.

Portofino is a romantic fishing village, situated partly on a small headland, partly in a little bay favoured by the English in the nineteenth century, and now beloved of rich yachtsmen. The many trees combine charmingly with the gay little houses.

Central Italy

*R*emoved but not cut off from the hustle and bustle of Rome and Milan, central Italy makes for an unusually pleasant visit to suit all tastes. Art lovers will appreciate Florence—the birthplace of the Renaissance—as well as many other towns in the area filled with artistic treasures. Food lovers will enjoy Bologna, the gastronomical capital of Italy. Those with an interest in religion will be attracted to Umbria, the birthplace of many saints: Francis, Clare, Valentine, and Benedict. All are set within a landscape that ranges from mountains to plains and coastal areas and features deliciously varied regional cuisines.

Emilia-Romagna

Emilia-Romagna as a political entity dates from the unification of Italy of the last century. As its name attests, however, it was known to the ancient Romans, whose Via Emilia ran, indeed still runs, from Piacenza to Rimini. Romagna is the eastern portion of the region; its principal city, Ravenna, was the capital of the Western Roman Empire and later became property of the popes, while the history of Emilia is rather more chequered, having passed from Guelph to Ghibelline, powerful family to powerful family, and between France and Austria before finally joining a unified Italy in 1860.

Bustling Bologna is the most important city in the region. Known to the Etruscans and later colonised by the Romans, its importance dates back at least as far as the thirteenth century, when the oldest university in Europe was founded there, earning the city the epithet 'Bologna La Dotta' (the Learned). Other sobriquets for Bologna are 'La Grassa' (The Fat, a reference to its role as the gastronomical capital of Italy), 'La Città dei Portici' (The City of Arches, a reference to the many evocative covered passageways that crisscross the city), and 'La Turrita' (The Towered).

Though this last name was given to Bologna when there were some 180 towers, only the Torre degli Asinelli and the Torre Garisenda remain, and both are leaning.

Bolognese architecture is characterised by the lavish use of brick, as can be seen in the Piazza Maggiore and Piazza del Nettuno, so called after the fountain of Neptune designed by native son Giambologna. Bologna's cathedral dates from the tenth century, though it has been rebuilt throughout the centuries. Another extensive building is the Gothic Palazzo Comunale, which houses the Municipal Art Gallery. The Museo Civico Archeologico has treasures from nearby Etruscan sites along with an important Egyptian collection and a fifth century BC head of Athena Lemnia. The Pinacoteca Nazionale houses an important collection of paintings, among which is *Saint Cecilia*, a masterpiece by Raphael. Also of note is the beautiful Gothic Mercanzia, home of the Chamber of Commerce.

A few simple pots of geraniums decorate this window and balcony in Pisa.

Olive trees cover the region of Tuscany, reputed to produce the finest Italian olive oil, especially the area near Lucca.

*Previous page:
Harvesting hay is
still done by the
old methods in this
Tuscan scene, in
which a simple
cart is pulled by
two white oxen.*

*Castiglione della
Pescaia, a well-
known resort of
the Maremma in
Tuscany, rises
on the site of the
ancient Roman
Salebro. It has
a castle and old
walls, but is pri-
marily known for
its sandy beaches.*

*Sunset at
Castiglione
della Pescaia.*

Bologna's sacred architecture is dominated by the church of San Petronio, the largest in the city, with sculpture by Jacopo della Quercia on the main doorway of the façade and a magnificent Gothic interior. Other fine churches are San Domenico, with an interior remodelled in baroque style and a tomb of St Dominic by Niccolò Pisano; Santo Stefano, a complex of eight buildings containing a lovely two-story cloister; Santa Maria dei Servi, with a beautiful portico; San Giacomo Maggiore, which contains the *Tomb of Antonio Bentivoglio* by Jacopo della Quercia and a *Virgin Enthroned* by Francesco Francia; and the lovely Gothic church of San Francesco. Just outside town is Monte della Guardia, at the end of a lengthy colonnade. It attracts visitors with its beautiful views extending as far as the Adriatic and the Apennines.

Ravenna is one of the most unusual cities in Italy. Much prized for its protected location in the midst of marshland, it served as the capital of the Western Roman Empire beginning in AD 404, when Emperor Flavius Honorius moved his court there from Milan. At the fall of the empire it was the capital of Italy under Odoacer; when he was murdered, Theodoric the Great further embellished the city. The Ostrogoths were then driven out under Justinian by the Byzantine general Belisaurus and became the seat of a Byzantine governor. The Lombards put an end to the Byzantine governorship in the eighth century. After being ruled by the Ghibelline

Crowded Rimini is the largest resort town on the Adriatic, popular with British and German vacationers. Its old town houses a Roman bridge, the Ponte d'Augusto, and the Tempio Malatestano, one of the outstanding productions of the Renaissance.

Polenta family, Ravenna briefly belonged to Venice until the sixth century, when it became part of the Papal States. Thereafter, in 1860, it joined a newly united Italy.

Much remains of Ravenna's glorious past. In the sixth-century church of San Vitale are magnificent mosaics honoring Justinian and his wife Theodora, along with Christ flanked by archangels and Saints Vitalis and Ecclesius. The mausoleum of Galla Placidia contains striking mosaics on a dark blue ground. The baptistery of San Giovanni in Fonte houses some of the oldest mosaics in Ravenna. The Archbishop's Palace features lovely mosaics from the sixth and seventh centuries. Mosaics in the church of Sant'Apollinare Nuovo depict views of Ravenna and the nearby port of Classis (where the largest and best preserved basilica in Ravenna, Sant'Apollonaire, is found). The baptistery of the Arians has sixth-century mosaics depicting the baptism of Christ. The tomb of Theodoric is a monumental two-story rotunda, most likely built under orders of Theodoric himself. Literati will appreciate another tomb in Ravenna, that of Dante, who died there in exile.

Another rewarding destination, Ferrara reached its zenith under the rule of the Este family, who commissioned much art and architecture. In the Palazzo Schifanoia are frescoes painted by the three painters who first formed the School of Ferrara: Cosme Tura, Ercole de' Roberti, and Francesco del Cossa. The Castello Estense houses frescoes by pupils of Dosso Dossi. Palazzo di Ludovico il Moro contains antique Greek and Etruscan vases excavated from nearby Spina. The Palazzina di Marfisa d'Este and the Casa Romei also contain collections of paintings and decorative arts.

Parma, famed for its cheese and ham, is also known as the town where the painter Antonio Allegri, called Correggio, lived and worked in the early sixth century. His masterpiece is a fresco entitled *The Assumption of the Virgin* in the dome of the twelfth-century cathedral. (The cathedral also houses works by sculptor Benedetto Antelami, who designed the adjacent baptistery as well.) More works by Correggio are to be seen in the Palazzo della Pilotta, an unfinished brick building begun in the sixth century. The Galleria Nazionale is housed there. In addition to works by Correggio, it also counts works by such great painters as Tiepolo and El Greco in its collection. On the same floor as the galleries is the grand Teatro Farnese, built for the ruling

San Michele di Pagana, on the Italian riviera in Liguria, is a resort town that also boasts a church containing The Crucifixion by Van Dyck.

Farnese family. The Teatro Reggio, built at the beginning of the last century, today is famous for attracting a very discerning audience to its opera productions. Music lovers will also wish to visit the birthplace of Arturo Toscanini, now a museum.

More Correggio frescoes are to be seen in the Camera di San Paolo, the dining hall of a former nunnery, as well as in the church of San Giovanni Evangelista. Other sights in Parma include the baroque church of the Santissima Annunziata and the Palazzo Ducale overlooking the Parco Ducale.

When Marie Louise, the Hapsburg wife of the Emperor Napoleon, ruled Parma, she created a perfume industry around the town's beautifully scented violets. Today it is still flourishing, and the violets may be purchased crystallised for eating, as well as in soaps and sachets.

The sixth-century church of San Vitale in Ravenna, is renowned for its magnificent mosaics. Its most famous mosaic depicts Christ flanked by archangels and Saints Vitalis and Ecclesius.

The Palazzo Vecchio just after sunset in Florence, when the city proudly illuminates many of its major monuments.

San Gimignanello, one of many tiny towns that are sprinkled throughout the Tuscan countryside.

Tuscany

To many, Tuscany represents the very picture of Italy. Here is an undulating landscape where cypresses alternate with olive orchards and vineyards, where medieval hilltop castles overlook venerable country villas, where the Renaissance was born and the purest Italian is spoken. Add to these a simple, hearty regional cuisine and the result is the perfect Italian region.

Florence, though known to the Romans, came into its own at the beginning of the twelfth century, when the wool and silk industries made it the most important town in central Italy. Crafts guilds gradually attained power, gaining control of the city government until the Medici took over. It was under Cosimo and Lorenzo the Magnificent that the city achieved unprecedented prominence in art and scholarship. Except for two periods when they were forced into exile, the Medici ruled Florence until the line became extinct in the eighteenth century. It then passed on to the house of Lorraine, which ruled (with a brief interruption by Napoleon) until 1860, when Tuscany became part of the newly united kingdom of Italy. Florence was the capital of Italy from 1865 to 1870. Not much remains of Florence's Roman days, save the names of the Roman buildings that once stood on them—the baths were on Via delle Terme, the capitol on Via del Campidoglio.

There is, however, considerable evidence of the city's medieval past. Most impressive is the Palazzo Vecchio, also known as the Palazzo della Signoria. Originally built to house and protect the ministry of the republican government (the Signoria), it was then inhabited by Cosimo I, who commissioned Giorgio Vasari to decorate it.

The cupola of the
Florence cathedral
of Santa Maria del
Fiore rises majestically
over the town, domi-
nating the skyline.

Michelangelo's unblushing white marble
David stands in its own special niche
at Florence's Galleria dell'Accademia.
It has been housed there since 1873,
when it was moved from the Piazza
della Signoria, where a copy now stands.

Among the building's treasures are Verrocchio's bronze *Putto* (in the Cancelleria), Donatello's *Judith and Holofernes* (in the Sala dell'Udienza), Michelangelo's *Victory* (in the Salone dei Cinquecento), and Giambologna's *Virtue Overcoming Vice* (also in the Salone dei Cinquecento). Still used as City Hall, the Palazzo della Signoria and the piazza of the same name that it overlooks still comprise the centre of Florentine life.

Another medieval structure, the Loggia dei Lanzi, is on the south side of the Piazza della Signoria. Designed for public ceremonies, today it houses a rich collection of statues, among which are Benvenuto Cellini's *Perseus* and Giambologna's *Rape of the Sabine Women* and *Hercules Slaying the Centaur*.

Likewise, another medieval building, called the Bargello, or Museo Nazionale, houses the most important collection of Renaissance sculpture in the world. Among its highlights are works by Michelangelo, Cellini, Giambologna, Donatello, and the Della Robbia family.

One of the oldest structures in Florence is also one of the most famous: the Ponte Vecchio. It was rebuilt in 1354 after repeated destruction, on the narrowest point of the Arno River in Florence. This is most likely where it was crossed by the Via Cassia, the ancient road that ran through Florence on its

Mosaics in Florence's octagonal baptistery of San Giovanni. Remarkably well preserved, they date from around 1225. The huge figure of Christ, attributed to Coppo di Marcovaldo, dominates from its position above the apse.

The Cantoria, made in the 1430s by Luca Della Robbia, originally stood in Florence's cathedral but is now in the city's Museo dell'Opera del Duomo. It portrays children dancing, singing, and playing musical instruments.

Views (here and next page) of the interior of the cathedral of Santa Maria del Fiore in Florence.

The interior of Florence's cathedral of Santa Maria del Fiore seems remarkably bare and chilly after the warmth of the exterior colour, but the marvellous marble pavement designed by Baccio d'Agnolo and others adds a touch of excitement.

way from Rome to Fiesole and Pisa, important cities in those days. Originally where butchers, tanners, and other practitioners of the 'vile arts' (as Ferdinand I de'Medici called them) set up shop, they were replaced by goldsmiths and jewellers in the sixth century. During the German retreat in World War II, the Ponte Vecchio was the only bridge Fascist troops could not bring themselves to blow up. Instead, they reduced buildings on either side of the bridge to rubble, rendering the Ponte Vecchio impassable. Another structure dating from medieval times is Orsanmichele. Occupying the site of the eighth-century oratory of San Michele in Orto, the Gothic building's ground floor was a covered market, while its upper floor housed a communal granary. The ruling Guelph party commissioned various guilds to decorate the exterior.

Colour gradually worked its way into the palette of Florentine architects. A prime example is the inlaid green-and-white marble used on the church of San Miniato al Monte, a delightful expression of eleventh- and twelfth-century Tuscan Romanesque. Dating from slightly later is the church of Santa Maria Novella, which uses a similar combination of green and white marble. Inside the church are frescoes by Domenico Ghirlandaio and others in the Cappellonedegli Spagnoli. Another example of coloured marble is to be found in Florence's Baptistery, famous for its three gilded bronze doors with relief decoration (one of which Michelangelo called 'the Gates of Paradise'). This octagonal structure was built during the eleventh to thirteenth centuries on the site of a Roman building.

Also making lavish use of coloured marble is the Gothic bell-tower, but it is the cathedral of Santa Maria del Fiore that is Florence's tour-de-force. This magnificent building takes its name from the lily, which is the emblem Florence. It was begun by Arnolfo di Cambio in 1296, but the facade was only completed during the last century. The façade dazzles with red marble from the Maremma, white from Carrara, and green from Prato. Its crowning glory came in the fifth century, when Filippo Brunelleschi designed the octagonal dome, which has since become the most important landmark of Florence. Its museum displays Michelangelo's splendid *Pietà*.

This figure, depicting the grotesque pot-bellied dwarf Morgante, Cosimo's court jester, astride a turtle, is but one example of the delightful statuary found in Florence's Boboli Gardens.

Statuary and fountains at Florence's Boboli Gardens, laid out for Cosimo I dei Medici by Tribolo and perhaps also by Ammannati after 1550, and extended in the early seventeenth century. They comprise the largest public park in the centre of Florence.

Bartholomeo Ammannati's Neptune Fountain in Florence's Piazza della Signoria. Much derided by Florentines, it gave rise to the taunt 'Ammannato, Ammannato, che bel marmo hai rovinato', or 'What beautiful marble you've ruined'.

The façade of the cathedral of Santa Maria del Fiore in Florence, completed only during the last century, matches that of the much older bell tower, begun by Giotto in 1334 and completed by Francesco Talenti in 1359.

Another view of Florence's cathedral of Santa Maria del Fiore and bell tower shows the three distinct colours of marble used in its construction: white from Carrara, green from Prato, and red from the Maremma.

Among other noteworthy churches in Florence are the church of Santa Trinita, one of the oldest Gothic churches in Italy; the church of San Lorenzo, which serves as a backdrop to a colourful outdoor market and was partially designed by Brunelleschi and Michelangelo (who was also responsible for the New Sacristy, the adjacent mausoleum of the Medici family); the church of the Santissima Annunziata, with frescoes by Andrea del Sarto; the church of Santa Croce, which contains the tombs of such famous Italians as Michelangelo, Machiavelli, and Galileo, as well as glorious frescoes. This stands adjacent to Brunelleschi's perfectly proportioned Pazzi Chapel. Among other important buildings are the church of Santo Spirito, also by Brunelleschi; the church of Santa Maria del Carmine, which contains the Brancacci Chapel, where stunning fifth-century frescoes by Masolino, Masaccio, and Filippino Lippi are to be found; and the monastery of San Marco, replete with charming frescoes by Fra Angelico.

Near to San Marco is the Accademia di Belle Arti, known for perhaps what is the most famous sculpture in the world, Michelangelo's *David*, which stands in bright white marble glory. Also in the vicinity is Florence's Archaeological Museum, which boasts extensive Etruscan and Egyptian collections.

One of the world's great art collections is under the roof of the Uffizi, originally built as government offices, but today a treasure trove of Florentine painting, as well as major works by northern Italian (particularly Venetian) painters. Outstanding pictures by Dutch and German masters are also part of the collection. Florence's other great museum is housed in the Palazzo Pitti, which displays works by Raphael, Andrea del Sarto, and Titian, among others, along with the former royal apartments and collections of precious objects. Adjacent to the Palazzo Pitti are the spectacular Boboli gardens, which lead to the Forte di Belvedere, which afford lovely views of Florence, as does the Piazzale Michelangelo.

Florence also abounds in good restaurants where Tuscan cuisine—ranging from *pappa al pomodoro* (a soup of tomato, bread, olive oil, onions, and basil) to *bistecca all fiorentina* to exquisite pecorino cheese desserts.

Once a great maritime republic, Pisa was an important city long before the Renaissance. Though little remains of its former glory, there are some noteworthy sights, including the church of Santa Maria della Spina; the church of Santo Stefano dei Cavalieri (it has a spectacular wooden ceiling by Giorgio Vasari); the Palazzo dell'Orologio; and two excellent museums, the Museo Nazioanle di San Matteo and the Museo dell'Opera del Duomo. But its most famous landmark remains the Leaning Tower, which is situated in the Campo dei Miracoli nearby a substantial cathedral (its apse mosaic is Giovanni Cimabue's last work) and a lovely baptistery.

Siena is one of Tuscany's most welcoming cities. *Cor magis tibi Siena pandit*—'To you Siena opens her heart even wider'—reads the Latin inscription on the city gate called Porta Camolla,

A view of Florence's cathedral dome, built by Filippo Brunelleschi from 1420 to 1436, as well as the bell tower begun by Giotto in 1334 when he was the most distinguished Florentine architect (as well as appointed city architect).

A copy of Andrea del Verrocchio's
bronze Putto (the original is
upstairs in the Cancelleria)
graces the entrance to Florence's
Palazzo Vecchio. Verrocchio
was Leonardo da Vinci's teacher.

and the message is true. With grace and civility, Siena has been opening its heart to the world for centuries.

Siena opened the way for painting as well. In the fourteenth century came Duccio di Buoninsegna, a painter whose stylistic influences included Nicola and Giovanni Pisano, Pisan sculptors who were working on the pulpit of Siena's famed cathedral at the time. Duccio's masterpiece is undoubtedly the *Maestà*, or *Majestic Madonna*. It hangs in the Museo dell'Opera del Duomo. After Duccio came the turn of his star pupil, Simone Martini, whose own version of the *Maestà* is in the Palazzo Pubblico. When Martini left for Avignon and the seat of the papacy, the two brothers Ambrogio and Pietro Lorenzetti had their turn as master painters of the Sienese Republic. Ambrogio left his *Allegory of Good and Bad Government* in the Palazzo Pubblico.

The evolution of Sienese painting is apparent from work at the Pinacoteca Nazionale, whose collection ranges from stiffly painted Byzantine Madonnas to a more humane Renaissance sensibility in works by such painters as Giovanni di Paolo, Matteo di Giovanni, and Il Vecchietta. The museum also displays the first pure landscapes to be painted in Europe, *City by the Sea* and *Castle on the Shore of a Lake*, both by Ambrogio Lorenzetti. Among many recurrent themes on view in the museum is that of Saint Catherine of Siena, who lived in Siena and is also venerated in the church of San Domenico.

Life in Siena revolves around the Piazza del Campo. It comes especially alive July 2 and August 16 each year with the Palio, an impassioned horse race dating from the Middle Ages. At other times of the year visitors can appreciate the sheer beauty of the piazza and its lovely copy of a fountain by Jacopo della Quercia.

The imposing
tower of the
Palazzo Vecchio,
built in 1310 to
designs tradition-
ally attributed to
Arnolfo di Cambio.
The tower was the
tallest building in
Florence until the
fifteenth century.

Umbria/Le Marche

'The green heart of Italy', as Umbria is known, is filled with ancient towns rising over a mystical landscape replete with the memories of numerous saints. Adjacent Le Marche, with its principal tourist city of Urbino, also boasts a proud past. Together they make a very pleasant venue for the visitor.

Like much of central Italy, Umbria was once occupied by the Etruscans. Numerous artifacts may be seen at the Museo Archeologico Nazionale dell'Umbria in Perugia, one of the original twelve cities that made up the Etruscan league. Near the museum is more recent evidence of a splendid past: the ninth-century Basilica of San Pietro, filled with masterful works of art by such painters as Perugino (*Pietà*) and Caravaggio (*Saint Francesca Romana*).

Another important monument in Perugia is the Rocca Paolina, the famous fort designed by Sangallo for Pope Paul III in the sixteenth century to help control the unruly Baglioni family. Nearby is the Oratorio di San Bernardino, dedicated to the fifteenth-century Sienese Franciscan preacher. Also worth a visit is the Palazzo dei Priori, a Gothic palace that once housed the city's ruling magistrates but today is the site of the Galleria Nazionale dell'Umbria, a museum displaying works by Piero della Francesca and, more locally, Perugino and Pinturicchio.

Pisa's splendid Campo dei Miracoli, a testament to Pisan wealth and power going back well before the Renaissance, houses not only the Leaning Tower but also the cathedral and baptistery, which date from the eleventh and twelfth centuries.

The Leaning Tower, the main attraction of Pisa. Begun in 1173, the tower was only a few metres high when a subsidence of the soil threw it out of perpendicular. In 1350 it was completed by Tommaso di Andrea da Pontedera.

As it flows through Pisa, the Arno River passes the little church of Santa Maria della Spina. It is a gem of a Pisan Gothic church, named for a thorn of the Saviour's crown, the gift of a Pisan merchant.

The Torre del Mangia casts a long shadow in Siena's Piazza del Campo. It unfolds in nine segments around a copy of Jacopo della Quercia's Fonte Gaia fountain.

'The Siena of today is a mere shrunken semblance of the rabid little republic which in the thirteenth century waged triumphant war with Florence, cultivated the arts with splendour, planned a cathedral of proportions almost unequalled', wrote Henry James.

Perugia is the best place to sample the robust cuisine of Umbria, from the tiny lentils of Castellucio to *gobbi* (fried cardoons), *porchetta alla perugina* (roasted suckling pig with fennel, rosemary, and garlic), *palombacci* (roasted wood pigeon), *mazzafegato* (a salami made with pork livers, pine nuts, raisins, orange peel, and sugar), and pungent black truffles. In a long tradition that dates from the days when the popes levied a tax on salt, the bread is not salted.

Assisi, where Saint Francis was born and ministered, is one of the treasures of Italy. Spread out over Monte Subasio, it has a gentle, mystical, rosy glow, which comes from the local pink stone. Assisi is dominated by its basilica, a two-storied structure built over Saint Francis's tomb in two different styles: the squat lower church is late Romanesque and the upper is Gothic (the first of its kind in Italy). The walls are covered with frescoes by Cimabue, Martini, Giotto, and Pietro Lorenzetti. In Assisi's main square, the Piazza del Comune, is a former ancient Roman temple. Once called the Temple of Minerva, it is now the church of Santa Maria della Minerva. Other striking sights are the cathedral façade and the Gothic church of Santa Chiara, which contains the open tomb of the founder of the Poor Clares. Also noteworthy in Assisi is the Rocca Maggiore, a castle in which Emperor Frederick II spent some time in this youth.

Pageantry precedes the Gioco del Calcio in Costume, an annual event in Florence in which players from each of Florence's four quartieri, or districts, play an antique from of soccer in authentic Renaissance costume.

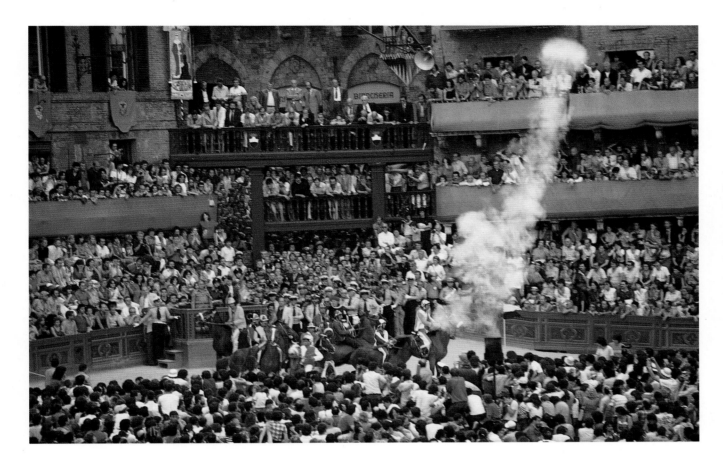

Pomp and circumstance abound twice a year when Siena runs its fabled horse race, the Palio. Rivalries run deep as seventeen contrade, or 'districts', compete for the prize, a palio, or 'cloth trophy'.

Volterra's medieval side is recalled during this pageantry taking place in the Piazza dei Priori, bordered by medieval mansions or mansions built in medieval style, including the Palazzo dei Priori, the oldest building of its kind in Tuscany.

San Gimignano's profile looks very much like a medieval Manhattan with its towers rising high in the sky. Such towers once proliferated in towns throughout Italy; San Gimignano has preserved more than any other place.

Elba, one of the islands in the Tuscan archipelago favoured by vacationers. Known since ancient times, it was famous for its iron ore, mentioned by Virgil, and more recently as Napoleon Bonaparte's place of exile.

A simple Tuscan farm, complete with the cypress trees that characterise so much of the Tuscan landscape.

Mysterious Volterra is 'on a towering great bluff of rock that gets all the winds and sees all the world', wrote D.H. Lawrence. Once a busy Etruscan city, some of its intrigue can still be sensed at dusk.

San Gimignano's medieval splendour is accentuated by nighttime illumination. Here aglow are vaults, a church, and some of the town's towers. Thirteen towers still survive out of some seventy-six tradition- ally thought to have existed.

The town of Cortona was a flourishing little township well before the Etruscans colonised it. During the Renaissance, it basked in the reflected glory of its most famous native son, painter Luca da Cortona or Luca Signorelli.

Another major city in Umbria is Spoleto, where the Festival of Two Worlds, a famous international performing arts event, takes place each summer. Its cathedral contains frescoes by Fra Filippo Lippi, who is also buried in the cathedral. Two museums worth a visit are the Museo Civico and the Pinacoteca in the Palazzo Comunale. The brooding Rocca, built in the fourteenth century as a papal residence, today is used as a prison. Built at the same time was the Ponte delle Torri, an imposing aqueduct and viaduct. Additionally, the churches of San Gregorio Maggiore and San Salvadore are not to be missed.

Even more imposing is Orvieto, magnificently situated on a tufa crag that rears up dramatically above a wide river valley. Oriveto is famous for its cathedral, one of the most splendid examples of Italian Gothic architecture, which houses frescoes by Fra Angelico and Luca Signorelli in its Cappella della Madonna di San Brizio. Opposite the cathedral is the Museo Archeologico Faina (in the Palazzo Faina) with its collection of Greek and Etruscan artifacts. On the east side of town are the remains of an Etruscan temple, as well as the sixteenth-century Well of San Patrizio, with two spiral staircases, one for descending and the other for ascending.

Just east of Umbria is Le Marche, a mountainous region that also extends to a generous slice of sea-coast along the Adriatic, the two circumstances that determine its cuisine. The mountains offer simply prepared lamb, pork, and veal dishes; the coast is a good place to sample *brodetto*, a type of fish soup, as well as any one of a number of local sea creatures.

The best known city in Le Marche is Urbino, settled by the Umbrians centuries before Christ.

Agriculture still plays an important role in the economy of Umbria, as seen by the meticulously ploughed field here outside the town of Foligno.

Assisi, the city of St Francis, rises mystically and majestically on an imposing spur of Monte Subasio. The mountain is made of a pink limestone, from which the entire city gets its unified character.

Following page: Perched on a giant upthrust of reddish tufa rock, a jagged remnant of volcanic days, Orvieto overlooks the wide valley of the river Paglia, appearing almost as a mirage.

Some of the lavish interior fresco decoration of Orvieto cathedral.

Frescoes by Luca Signorelli in Orvieto cathedral. Originally commissioned from Benozzo Gozzoli, who was recalled to Rome, the frescoes completed by Signorelli are among the most remarkable of the Italian Renaissance.

Orvieto cathedral is one of the most striking buildings of its period in Italy. Its construction was ordered by Pope Urban IV to commemorate the miracle of Bolsena. The first stone was laid on November 13, 1290, when it was blessed by Nicholas IV.

It became a Roman municipality in the third century BC, but its true heyday came during the fifteenth century under Duke Federico di Montefeltro, whose court was considered to be the most enlightened of its day. Today the city's main attraction is the Palazzo Ducale, the most perfectly preserved example of an Italian princely residence of the Renaissance. It contains a throne room filled with Gobelin tapestries and a study that is a great exercise in trompe l'oeil. The palazzo also houses the Galleria Nazionale delle Marche, where native son Raphael's *The Mute* is on display, along with works by Piero della Francesca and Paolo Uccello. Raphael himself is commemorated by his birthplace at Via Raffaello 57.

Fine artwork by another of Urbino's native sons, Federigo Barocci, is found at the cathedral. It was rebuilt in 1801 after the destruction of an earlier church in 1789. Nearby in the Oratorio di San Giovanni are frescoes depicting the life of Saint John the Baptist by Lorenzo and Jacopo Salimbeni.

A contemporary sculpture by Giacomo Manzu contrasts with historic architecture in Spoleto, site of the Festival of Two Worlds, an annual summer extravaganza of music, dance, and theatre.

Urbino, one of the principal cities of the Le Marche region, reached the height of its influence during the fifteenth century, when under the great **condottiere Federico da Montefeltro,** *one of the great cultural centres of all time was created.*

*Men and women alike take part in
the tobacco harvest outside Umbria.*

*Gubbio, a quintessentially medieval town,
has remained well preserved due to its
remoteness and relative inaccessibility.
A medieval Disneyland, Gubbio provides
visitors with a taste of the mysterious,
mythical, and earthy all at the same time.*

Rome

*F*or the first-time visitor, Rome is a confusing jumble of buildings spanning two thousand years of history around which traffic speeds like a whirlwind no matter what the time of day. That impression is correct. But there is a method to the madness. With a little prodding, Rome gently and gradually reveals itself in all its glory, from the ancient monuments of the Roman Forum through medieval and baroque churches right down to the most modern-day suburbs.

The Heart of the City

Between the deep red of the ancient brick and the stark white of modern marble and concrete are the mellower tones, now fixed by law, of its palazzos and villas. The colours are made even more striking in combination with the stately Renaissance style imported from Florence or the exuberant baroque style born in Rome and favoured by the popes. Rome's present look is a blend of all such styles, with a touch (but just a touch) of order added when the government of a newly united Italy lined the Tiber with travertine embankments as the Eternal City became its capital.

That was in the last century, but Rome was the capital of an empire centuries before that, when the Tiber meandered through the city of seven hills (the Palatine, Capitoline, Aventine, Celian, Esquiline, Viminal, and Quirinal) on its left bank. Today, as it has been since the eleventh century, the Capitoline (Campidoglio in Italian) is the seat of Rome's municipal government. It rises behind Italy's largest monument, the Victor Emmanuel II, which dominates Piazza Venezia, where stands the Palazzo di Venezia, the earliest Renaissance palace in Rome. In the adjacent Palazzetto di Venezia is the Museo del Palazzo di Venezia, the only decorative arts museum in Rome. Also nearby is the church of San Marco, which boasts a fine interior.

Piazza del Campidoglio, designed by Michelangelo, crowns the Campidoglio. On it are Palazzo Senatorio, the official seat of the Mayor of Rome; the Palazzo del Museo Capitolino, which houses an impressive collection of Roman sculpture; and the Palazzo dei Conservatori, which comprises three museums, the Saladei Conservatori, the Museo del Palazzo dei Conservatori, and the Pinacoteca. Nearby, on the highest spot of the Campidoglio, is the ancient church of Santa Maria in Aracoeli.

Also from the Campidoglio is the best view of the Roman Forum, the heart of ancient Rome. The Forum is a formidable

Piazza Navona, one of the liveliest places in Rome, surrounds the Fountain of the Four Rivers by Bernini, which makes poetic use of realistic objects symbolic of Rome itself.

This late-night cafe provides refreshment to Romans and visitors alike. Open until the wee hours, the cafe is an important part of everyday life in Rome, the meeting place for the exchange of ideas and gossip.

piece of real estate, encompassing over a thousand years of development and meeting political, legal, and commercial needs. It is best appreciated with the help of a guidebook (there are always some on sale outside the entrance at the end of the Via Cavour), but its main features instantly come to life with the help of a little imagination. The arch of Septimius Severus, the Temple of Antoninus and Faustina, the Basilica of Maxentius, and the Arch of Titus are among the most prominent landmarks in the Forum.

On leaving the Forum it makes a pleasant stroll to the Circus Maximus. Though it has been pillaged throughout the centuries, reducing it to an oblong field, the site is still evocative of the times when four chariots raced together for seven laps, watched by a crowd of 385,000 people. Nearby is the Arch of Constantine, the largest and best preserved of the ancient arches. Also within walking distance is the Colosseum, perhaps the most famous building in the world. With a seating capacity of fifty thousand spectators, it was *not* where Christians were fed to the lions, but rather the place where gladiators fought. South of the Colosseum are the ruins of the Baths of Caracalla, which provide a dramatic backdrop for Rome's summer opera season. Across the Via dei Fori Imperali, built by Mussolini as a triumphal highway, are forums laid out by successive emperors. Caesar's Forum, mostly on the Roman Forum side of the avenue, contains Trajan's column. Trajan's Forum includes Trajan's Market as well. Beyond it are the Forum of Augustus and the Forum of Nerva.

Back at the Campidoglio, on Via del Teatro di Marcello, is the Teatro di Marcello, otherwise known as the Palazzo Orsini, after the family who inhabit the apartments above. The Arch of Janus is just a bit farther, as are the church of San Giorgio in Velabro, named for the marsh in which Romulus and Remus were found, and, adjoining it, the Arch of the Money Lenders. On the other side of the boulevard are the round marble Temple of Vesta and the Temple of Fortuna Virilis. At the end of the street

An ancient statue depicts the she wolf suckling the twin brothers Romulus and Remus, who according to legend were rescued by her on the Palatine Hill. Thereafter, the legend goes, they founded Rome on April 21, 753 BC.

is the medieval church of Santa Maria in Cosmedin, known for the 'mouth of truth' (Bocca della Verità) on its porch: Telling a lie with one's hand stuck in the mouth is said to result in amputation. The church itself has a floor covered with charming mosaics made by the Cosmati.

Across the Via del Circo Massimo, a winding road from the Piazzale Romolo e Remo ascends the Aventine Hill to the church of Santa Sabina, a lovely fifth-century basilica with carved cypress doors, which portray one of the earliest representations of the Crucifixion. In the nearby Piazza dei Cavalieri di Malta is a keyhole (at no. 3) that gracefully frames St Peter's.

On the Via del Plebiscito is the Palazzo Doria Pamphili, which houses an outstanding art collection, including works by Titian, Michelangelo da Caravaggio, Diego Rodriguez de Silva Velázquez, and Giovanni Lorenzo Bernini. Nearby is Piazza della Minerva, with its confection of an elephant by Bernini supporting an obelisk on its back. The piazza takes its name from the church of Santa Maria Sopra Minerva, one of the few ancient Gothic churches in Rome, built on the site of a Temple to Minerva. Inside is a treasure trove of art, including Michelangelo's *Christ with the Cross*. Around the corner is the Pantheon, the first building ever conceived as an interior space. The inside, with its circular opening at the top, contains the tombs of Raphael and Vittoriò Emanuele II and Umberto I. The church of San Luigi dei Francesi contains dramatic canvases by Caravaggio, as does the church of Sant'Agostino, which also has works by Raphael and Bernini. Work by Bernini's rival, Borromini, may be seen nearby at the church of Sant'Ivo, where he designed the church and its courtyard.

Borromini and Bernini continue their feud in lovely Piazza Navona, where Borromini built the church of Sant'Agnese in Agone. In designing the Fountain of the Rivers facing it, Bernini made the figures avert their glances from the church. The two other fountains in the piazza, Moor Fountain and the Neptune Fountain, were made by Bernini and his school. A few streets away is

Roman domes abound during sunset as viewed from Trinita dei Monte at the top of the Spanish Steps.

the church of Santa Maria della Pace, which contains frescoes by Raphael and Bramante's earliest Roman creation, the cloisters. On the other side of Via del Corso is the famous Trevi Fountain, where tradition dictates a coin be tossed to ensure a return to Rome.

On the other side of town is the Villa Borghese, not a villa but a large park built on the Pincio Hill for Cardinal Scipione Borghese. The Villa Borghese is one of the greenest and most serene public places in Rome, a favourite spot for a picnic, a trip with the children to its modern zoo, or a promenade to its Piazzale Napoleon I on the west side of the Pincio for a traditional view of Rome over Piazza del Popolo. There are also a number of museums in the park. The Museo Borghese houses a collection of works by Bernini, Raphael, Caravaggio, and Titian. The Galleria Nazionale d'Arte Moderna has a fine collection of modern art by such painters as De Chirico, Boccioni, and Pistoletto, as well as some foreign works. The Museo Nazionale di Villa Giulia is known for its Etruscan collection.

From Villa Giulia, Via Flaminia leads to the grand gate called Porta del Popolo and the Piazza del Popolo. Immediately to the left is the church of Santa Maria del Popolo, which was constructed with funds from the *popolo* (people) and gives the piazza its name. Best known for its two paintings by Caravaggio, it also contains the Cappella Chigi designed by Raphael and works by Pinturicchio, Annibale Carracci, and Bernini. Across the piazza are the twin churches of Santa Maria di Montesanto and Santa Maria dei Miracoli, playful exercises in the art of illusionary design begun by Carlo Rainaldi. Santa Maria di Montesanto is narrower than Santa Maria dei Miracoli, so Rainaldi topped the former with an oval dome and the latter with a round one to make them look symmetrical, and they do. Between the two churches runs Via del Corso, named after the horse races that were run there during Carnival. On Via di Ripetta is the Ara Pacis Augustae, an altar finished in 9 BC to celebrate the Augustan peace. Across the street is the Mausoleum of Augustus, now stripped of its original travertine covering and obelisks.

Nearby is Piazza di Spagna, which takes its name from the Palazzo di Spagna at no. 57, the Spanish embassy to the Holy See. The Spanish Steps, which rise in the

The Spanish Steps, all 137 of them, provide a romantic way of scaling the hill to the French-built church of Trinità dei Monte. They also provide a place to stop and rest while sightseeing in the Eternal City.

Along with the adjacent Via Borgognona and Via Frattina, bustling Via dei Condotti (as seen here from the Spanish Steps) comprises the main shopping area of Rome and is filled with boutiques selling wares by Italy's most famous designers.

A statue of Lord Byron stands amidst the billowing umbrella pines of the Villa Borghese, a magnificent park created in the seventeenth century by Cardinal Scipione Borghese and covering an area over 6 kilometres (3.5 miles) in circumference.

The Arch of Titus, a beautifully proportioned triumphal arch erected in AD 81 to honor the victories of Titus and Vespasian in the Judean War. The arch is especially interesting for the sculptural reliefs on the inside surfaces.

The enormous Teatro Marcello (120 metres, or 393 feet, in diameter), was capable of holding twenty thousand spectators. Partially converted to a palazzo in the sixteenth century, today it is called Palazzo Orsini after the family who still inhabit it.

The Trevi Fountain, the most spectacular and famous of all Roman fountains, is a 1762 work by Niccolò Salvi. Tradition dictates that visitors toss a coin over their shoulders into the fountain to ensure a return to Rome.

Piazza Navona, considered by many to be the finest of Rome's piazzas, is an elongated 'square' occupying the site of the Circus Agonalis. Used in ancient times for athletic contests and displays, today it is an animated residential square.

Following page: At the Colosseum, spectators once witnessed the killing of wild beasts and criminals, as well as gladiator combat. This prompted the second-century satirist Juvenal to accuse the populace of having sold its power for 'bread and circuses'.

middle of the piazza, were actually paid for by the French to create an easier access to the church of Trinità dei Monti, built by their kings at the top of the hill. Keats lived and died in the house at no. 26 and is commemorated in the Keats Shelley Memorial there. In the southern triangle of Piazza di Spagna is the column dedicated to the Immaculate Conception, crowned each December 8 by the Pope. The building behind the column is the Palazzo di Propaganda Fide, the missionary centre of the Catholic world. Bernini and Borromini both worked on its façades at different times. The side facing the piazza is the work of Bernini, and his rival's concave façade is to the right.

Back at the base of the Spanish Steps is the Fontana della Barcaccia, a fountain by Pietro Bernini or possibly his more famous son, Gianlorenzo. From it, 137 steps lead to the church of Trinità dei Monti. The French occupy not only the church, but also the adjacent Villa Medici, where Louis XIV established the Académie de France and the Prix de Rome in 1666. Today its gardens are virtually unchanged. From there, Via Sistina leads to Piazza Barberini. The centrepiece of the piazza is the Triton Fountain by Bernini, and at the corner of the Via Veneto is his Fountain of the Bees. Just up the Via Veneto is the church of Santa Maria della Concezione, its five chapels decorated in bizarre rococo patterns formed by the bones of some four thousand Capuchin monks.

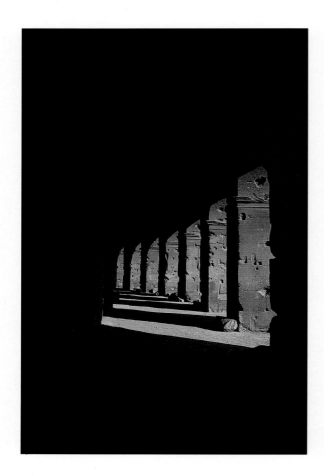

Used in combination with a system of barrel vaults, the Colosseum's circular tufa walls effectively solved the problem of coping with the building's formidable size and weight.

Three columns are all that remain of the Temple of Castor and Pollux in the Roman Forum. The temple was built in 484 BC by the dictator Aulus Postimius in honor of Castor and Pollux's miraculous appearance at the Battle of Lake Regillus.

Just off Piazza Barberini, on Via delle Quattro Fontane, is Palazzo Barberini, begun in 1625 by Carlo Maderno and then taken over by Borromini and Bernini. Today it houses the Galleria Nazionale d'Arte Antica, which is not a gallery of antique art at all, but rather an impressive collection of works by Fra Angelico, Caravaggio, Tintoretto, El Greco, and Raphael. Where Via delle Quattro Fontane intersects Via del Quirinale are the four fountains from which the street takes its name. This is also the crossroads of the wide streets laid out by Pope Sixtus V, with sweeping views leading to Porta Pia to the northeast, the obelisks of the Quirinal Hill to the southwest, the Esquiline Hill to the southeast, and Trinità dei Monti to the northwest. On the far corner of Via del Quirinale is Borromini's church of San Carlo alle Quattro Fontane, with a lovely adjacent cloister. The geometric complexity of the church's interior provides an obvious contrast to the interior of Bernini's church of Sant'Andrea al Quirinale just down the street, which is relatively simple in spite of its rich marble and gilt decor. Farther down the street is the Palazzo del Quirinale. Designed by Maderno, Bernini, and many others, it was formerly a summer residence of the popes and later used by the kings of Italy. Today it is occupied by the president of the republic.

The Colosseum is the greatest monument of ancient Rome. Despite its stupendous bulk, the building, which in its heyday could seat some fifty thousand spectators, is perfectly balanced due to the subtle use of spatial harmony and variation of architectural orders.

Nearby is the Piazza della Repubblica, with its tall spray of water shooting out of the Fontana delle Naiadi, an 1885 bronze fountain by Alessandro Guerrieri representing naiads cavorting with sea monsters. North of the piazza are the Baths of Diocletian, the largest of all the baths in Rome, able to accommodate three thousand people. Today, the church of Santa Maria degli Angeli is housed within the original Tepidarium. It was begun by Michelangelo, who converted the baths' vast central hall into the nave, but when Vanvitelli took over the design, he changed the nave into the transept. The church and its adjacent convent now house the Museo delle Terme di Diocleziano, displaying art from the late Roman Republic. Another important museum, the Museo Nazionale Romano, is close by in the Collegio Massimo.

After such extensive museum-going, the Roman visitor has certainly earned a good meal, and Rome's penchant for the table is legendary. Its roots go back to the Lucullus-style banquets satirised by Petronius in his *Satyricon* and recreated for the cinema by Federico Fellini in our time. Even today, nothing gives a Roman more pleasure than an outing at the local *osteria*—the simple neighbourhood eatery more abundant in Rome than anywhere else in Italy—for a loud and lengthy meal accompanied by many a *fujetta* (the glass carafe introduced by Pope Sixtus V) of Colli Albani wine.

The osteria is the essence of Roman dining, for the best restaurants in town are neither trendy nor fussy. The osteria traditionally serves such regional Roman dishes as *coda alla vaccinara* (oxtail stew), *rigatoni e pajata* (tubular pasta prepared with veal intestines), tripe, and sweetbreads. But there are a number of other Roman specialties served, for those who prefer, and it is highly recommended to experiment with new and unfamiliar dishes.

A view of the charmingly planted Roman Forum, with the Temple of Castor and Pollux in the foreground. In the distance are the church and bell tower of Santa Maria Nova (also known as Santa Francesca Romana) and the Colosseum.

The church of Santa Maria Nova (also known as Santa Francesca Romana) in the Roman Forum incorporates an Oratory of Saints Peter and Paul and contains a lovely twelfth-century bell tower. The facade, by Carlo Lombardi, dates from 1615.

A spectacular view from the roof of St Peter's reveals baroque statuary leading to the colonnades designed by Bernini. These, in turn, surround an obelisk brought to Rome from Alexandria.

The Via Appia Antica, or Appian Way, the most important of ancient Rome's consular roads, passes the Catacombs and ancient cemeteries on the way to Brindisi on the Adriatic coast, hundreds of miles away.

The Vatican

If all roads lead to Rome, they soon lead across the Tiber to the Vatican. Since 1929, when Mussolini and Cardinal Pietro Gaspari signed the Lateran Treaty between Italy and the Holy See, Vatican City—the seat of the Roman Catholic church and the cradle of all Christendom—has been an independent state ruled by papal authority, the only absolute sovereign in Europe. The Vatican, as it is most commonly known, has its own flag and national anthem, mints its own coinage, prints its own postage stamps (many Romans have more faith in its postal system than their own, and go to the Vatican just to mail their letters), has its own quarterly newspaper, radio station, and also plans for a television station.

In addition, a considerable part of the Vatican is taken up by St Peter's, the world's largest basilica in the world's smallest state. In addition to establishing the sovereign territory contained within the high walls of the Vatican, the Lateran Treaty granted special extraterritorial privileges to the churches of San Giovanni in Laterano, Santa Maria Maggiore, and San Paolo Fuori le Mura. Together with St Peter's, they constitute the four major basilicas of Rome.

The approach to the Vatican as envisioned by Bernini begins on Italian territory in Piazza Ponte Sant'Angelo across the Tiber from Castel Sant'Angelo. Walking over the bridge of Ponte Sant'Angelo, the Roman visitor is greeted by statues of the Saints Peter and Paul and virtually escorted by ten additional angel statues by Bernini.

Looking like a medieval flying saucer over the other side of the Tiber is the Castel Sant'Angelo. The ancient mausoleum of Hadrian, it was once landscaped, clad in travertine, covered with sculpture, and topped with a bronze statue of the emperor. In the Middle Ages it became part of the Aurelian Wall and a gate on the castle grounds called Porta San Pietro became the main point of entry to the

A large fountain splashes before the obelisk brought from Alexandria to St Peter's Square. In the background are the four-deep columns of Bernini's colonnade topped with a congenial array of statuary.

A rare moment before the crowds have begun to fill Piazza San Pietro. Here, Carlo Maderno's sumptuous facade dwarfs the dome originally designed by Michelangelo to be as prominent a feature close up as it is at a distance.

Vatican for religious pilgrims. On the top floor are the sumptuous papal apartments, from which, after a display of military paraphernalia, a passageway leads to a terrace familiar from the last act of *Tosca*, the one from which the heroine jumps to her death in the Tiber. The terrace has one of the best views of Rome and offers a closeup of the eighteenth-century statue of the Archangel Saint Michael.

In Bernini's day, a walk down the narrow medieval streets from Castel Sant'Angelo directly west through the area known as the Borgo led to the delightful surprise of his expansive piazza at St Peter's. Now, however, the grandiose Via della Conciliazione has ludicrously overextended the welcoming arms of Bernini's colonnade and ruined the dramatic element of turning into Piazza San Pietro. Nothing, however, can completely undermine the effects of Piazza San Pietro, an immense oval above which keep watch 140 stone saints on the colonnade and thirteen giant statues on the façade of St Peter's. The focal point of the piazza is the obelisk in the centre, flanked on either side by the jets of two baroque fountains. Between the fountains and the colonnades is a circle of black marble in the pavement, from which all four rows of colonnades appear to blend into one. The original St Peter's basilica, built on the site of the tomb of St Peter in 326 under Constantine, was a sumptuous early Christian edifice almost as large as the present one. When it began showing signs of age, the popes decided to build a new one and appointed a succession of architects for the task. Bramante, Raphael, Sangallo, Michelangelo, and others were involved at one point or another, and their designs alternately called for Greek- and Latin-cross plans. Michelangelo's design for a Greek cross and dome was being carried out at the time of his death in 1564, but under Paul V it was decided to conform to the outlines of Constantine's original basilica. This, unfortunately, makes Michalangelo's dome appear to sink as one approaches the entrance, although it is the glory of the Roman skyline from elsewhere in the city. Carlo Maderno designed the facade and portico (where Giotto's ceiling mosaic from the old basilica is installed) in an early baroque style. Embedded in the pavement is the porphyry disc atop which Pope Leo III crowned Charlemagne as Holy Roman Emperor in 800.

Inside, the effect is as dazzling as was intended. Perfect proportions mask the vastness of St Peter's, but spotting the minuscule forms of other visitors beneath the gigantic statues, or a look at the comparative lengths of other European churches, traced in metal in the floor of the nave, confirm its great size.

In the first chapel on the right is Michelangelo's *Pietà*. At the right end of the nave is Arnolfo di Cambio's bronze statue of *St Peter Enthroned*, its foot worn by the touches and kisses of the faithful over the centuries. Over the high altar soars Bernini's gilded bronze *baldacchino*, its four fluted columns spiralling up to support a canopy crowned by an orb and cross a hundred feet above the floor.

Bernini was entrusted with the decoration of the interior, and his works abound throughout. In the apse behind the baldacchino is his reliquary of the throne of

Looking very much like a medieval flying saucer, Castel Sant'Angelo keeps majestic watch over Rome and the Vatican from its privileged position at the end of Ponte Sant'Angelo, designed by Bernini as the first part of his approach to St Peter's.

St Peter's dominates the Roman skyline, seen here from behind Ponte Sant'Angelo, a bridge ornamented with Bernini's statues of Saints Peter and Paul, as well as ten joyous angels to herald one's visit to the Vatican.

114

St Peter, topped by a stained-glass representation of the Holy Spirit. His tomb of Alexander VII in the passage leading to the left transept is but one highlight among many magnificent monuments in the church. Back near Arnolfo's statue of St Peter is the entrance to the Vatican Grottoes, a dimly lit church containing a number of chapels and tombs. Beneath them are the famous excavations of what is believed to be the original tomb of St Peter, where in the 1940s an ancient crypt containing bones and the remains of a garment fitting the description of this legendary figure were discovered.

In the opposite direction, it is possible and highly recommended to visit the roof for a fascinating walk and closeup views of the gigantic statues on the façade. Inspired souls may then continue up the 537 steps to the lantern for a last inspirational view of the Vatican, Rome, the Alban Hills, and the surrounding countryside.

The perfect proportions of the interior of St Peter's basilica reveal its truly divine immensity when contrasted with the presence of mere mortals. Here, a shaft of light seems to be coming from heaven itself.

The grandeur of Michelangelo's dome of St Peter's is best appreciated from inside the basilica, since his original plan was changed as the apse was lengthened, effectively making much of the dome disappear when viewed from outside.

Southern Italy

*E*xcept for the area around Naples, southern Italy has been largely overlooked as a tourist destination. Happily, that situation is changing, for southern Italy holds many glorious surprises. In addition to the well-known Amalfi coast, Capri, and Ischia, there is much of interest to the visitor. The mountains of the Abruzzi, the theatricality of everyday life in Naples, the Apulian Romanesque cathedrals of Apulia, the refreshing outdoors of Calabria, and remnants of Greek colonies throughout, all make for a rewarding visit to a relatively undiscovered part of Italy.

The Abruzzi

The two regions of L'Abruzzo e il Molise combine to form an area called the Abruzzi. It is a mountainous place, where men and women still wear colourful peasant dress and believe in witches and *lupi mannari*, or werewolves. The modern world is making inroads, however, and the area now attracts nature lovers in the warmer months and skiers in the winter.

The largest city in the Abruzzi is L'Aquila, replete with architectural treasures from fine Romanesque and Renaissance churches to an imposing Spanish castello complete with moat. The castle is now occupied by the Museo Nazionale d'Abruzzo, which houses archaeological artifacts, Medieval art, and Renaissance sculpture. Two churches are also noteworthy, the Romanesque Santa

The gardens of the Palazzo Rufolo in Ravello, a charming stop along the Amalfi Drive. Here Wagner found inspiration for the magic garden of Klingsor in Parsifal; the palace also houses a small collection of antiquities.

Rising in an amphitheatre at the end of the Valley of the Dragone, the white town of Atrani is one of many lovely little towns along the scenic Amalfi Drive, which hugs the seacoast near the town of the same name.

Following page: The peaceful harbor in Bari's Città Vecchia, or Old Town, belies Bari's role as the major city in the region of Apulia, a bustling agricultural and commercial area renowned for its numerous annual trade fairs.

Maria di Collemaggio and the Renaissance church of San Bernardino, built for Saint Bernardino of Siena, who died in L'Aquila.

In the environs of L'Aquila are several sights worth seeing. In Bazzano is the lovely thirteenth-century church of Santa Giusta. Near the hill town of Castelnuovo are the ruins of Roman Peltunium, where there is also the eighth-century church of San Paolo. The little town of Caporciano has two of the most celebrated monuments in Christianity, the churches of Santa Maria Assunta and San Pelligrino. The mountain town of Teramo has a twelfth-century cathedral, as well as the church of Madonna della Grazie. Castelli, still known for its pottery, has its Museo delle Ceramiche di Castelli, a ceramics museum, as well as the elaborate tile ceiling of the church of San Donato. On the way to Atri are two more churches, San Clemente al Vomano and Santa Maria de Propezzano, while Atri itself boasts a thirteenth-century cathedral, a Palazzo Ducale, and the Museo Capitolare, housing an interesting collection of jewellery, ecclesiastical items, and wooden sculpture. San Pelino has a lovely Romanesque church. Pescocostanzo is a gabled medieval town; there, the church of Santa Maria del Colle boasts an exceptionally fine ceiling. Scanno is a hilltop town where each Sunday the town matrons don traditional clothing, headdresses, and all. Sulmona, the birthplace of the Roman poet Ovid, has the church of Santa Maria Annunziata, the cathdral of San Panfilo, and the Museo Civico, with its magnificent collection of jewellery. The other regional native son and poet is Gabriele d'Annunzio, born in the coastal town of Pescara. Roman ruins are to be seen in the towns of Alba Fucens and Chieti, where the Museo Nazionale Archeologico di Antichita has its collection of objects from antiquity. Near Chieti is the impressive Abbey of San Clemente a Casauria. In Molise, at the southern end of the Abruzzi, are excavations at Pietrabbondante and Saepinum, as well as the pristine town of Agnone.

Brienza, a sleepy little town in the
region of Basilicata, one of the poorest
and least-known regions in Italy.

*Morano Calabro, Calabria, in its splendid setting nestled in the foothills of
the Sila. It is dominated on its conical hill by the church of San Pietro, which
contains fine marble statues of Santa Caterina and Santa Lucia by Pietro Bernini.*

Outdoors lovers will want to see the Gran Sasso, a vast snow-capped ridge. Also in the area is the Parco Nazionale d'Abruzzo, a generous expanse of scenic splendour inhabited by chamois, bears, and golden eagles.

Campania

The best introduction to Naples is Spaccanapoli, where Saint Thomas Aquinas and Benedetto Croce both lived. Today, it bustles with life. Sights there include the church of Santa Chiara and its adjoining cloister, the church of San Domenico Maggiore, the Cappella San Severo, the church of Sant'Angelo, the church of San Gregorio Armeno, the church of San Lorenzo Maggiore and its adjacent museum, as well as the church of San Paolo Maggiore.

Naples's cathedral is renowned for the fact that its most holy artifact, the dried blood of the city's patron saint, San Gennaro, is said to miraculously liquefy twice a year—on September 19 and December 16, to be precise. Nearby is the church of Sant'Anna dei Lombardi.

Neapolitan museums include the Museo Archeologico Nazionale, which houses a spectacular collection of objects from Pompeii and Herculaneum; the Galleria Nazionale di Capodimonte, which has paintings by Bellini, Titian, Rubens, and Caravaggio; and the Certosa di San Martino, a fourteenth-century monastery that now houses examples of Naples's art of elaborate *presepi*, or nativity scenes; and the Museo Pignatelli, a neoclassical villa where carriages are displayed.

Other major monuments in Naples are the thirteenth-century castle, Castel Nuovo; the church of the Santissima Annunciata; the Teatro San Carlo, Italy's best-known opera house after La Scala in Milan, flanked by a Galleria; the Palazzo Reale; and the Castel dell'Ovo.

North of Naples are a number of interesting sights. Lake d'Averno, where Virgil located the Gates of

Hell, still evokes visions of the underworld. The Scavi di Baia are excavations of a Roman thermal spa and summer resort. At Cuma is the Sibyl of Cuma. Pozzuoli has extensive excavations on view. Caserta offers visitors the eighteenth-century Palazzo Reale, suggestive of Versailles. South of Naples lie the better known sites of Herculaneum, Paestrum, and Pompeii—destroyed by the volcanic eruption of Vesuvius in 79 AD.

Capri and Ischia are two resort islands in the Bay of Naples. Capri has the Villa Iovis, Tiberius's villa; the Torre del Faro, an ancient lighthouse; the Grotta Azurra, or 'blue grotto'; and the delightful little towns of Capri and Anacapri. Ischia is less developed than Capri, known for its little towns interspersed with white beaches and gentle seascapes.

The Amalfi Drive is one of the most spectacular drives in the world, curving along majestic cliffs terraced with vineyards and lemon groves, bordered by the rocky shore below. The sea views are as fresh as watercolours, splashed with pine and cactus and brightened by wild roses and bougainvillea. It begins in Sorrento, runs through cliffside Positano, Amalfi and its proud seafaring past and beautiful cathedral, graceful Ravello, and the ceramics town of Vietri sul Mare.

Often described as 'the heel of the Italian boot', the region of Apulia has had the heels of various peoples planted on its flat and vulnerable topography from the prehistoric times of the ancient Apuli tribes through Greeks, Romans, Byzantines, Lombards, Franks, Saracens, Normans, Hohenstaufens, Angevins, Aragonese, and Bourbons. Yet the region draws visitors not just because of its peculiar historical heritage (which left its mark on local art and architecture), but also for the natural wonders of its spectacular coastline, caves, and forests.

In the north of the region is the Foresta Umbra, the closest thing Italy has to an enchanted forest, an extensive forest of old beech, oak, pine, and chestnut trees. The same part of Apulia has the Santuario di San Michele, one of the most important religious sanctuaries in the Christian world.

Bustling Naples sprawls out along its bay. 'The most populous of cities relative to its size, whose luxurious inhabitants seem to dwell on the confines of paradise and hell-fire', observed Edward Gibbon in 1796.

Bari is Apulia's bustling seaport and the commercial and adminstrative centre of the region. Its Città Vecchia, or Old City, boasts a prototypical Apulian Romanesque church of San Nicola di Bari, housing an important bishop's throne as well as the tomb of St Nicholas. The Città Vecchia has another Frederick II castle. Points of interest outside the Old City are the Museo Archeologico, an important archaeological museum; the Pinacoteca Provinciale, an art museum housing an extensive collection of art from the eleventh to the nineteenth centuries; and the Teatro Petruzelli, Italy's third-ranking opera house after La Scala in Milan and San Carlo in Naples.

Inland from Bari, in the neighbouring region of Basilicata, is the town of Matera, famous for its

Fantastic trompe l'oeil fresco painting in Sorrento's cathedral. The town itself is no less fantastic, perched on a tufa rock high above the sea and bounded on three sides by deep ravines.

sassi, an extensive area of dwellings carved into the side of a ravine. To the southeast is another natural wonder, Castellana Grotte, the site of the largest and most spectacular caverns in Italy. A man-made wonder comes at Alberobello, a town with a central area of more than one thousand *trulli*—beehive-shaped structures used to house everything from farmers' tools to people. Three more towns complete the sightseeing in this part of Apulia: elegant Martina Franca, a baroque town whose Palazzo Ducale is the setting for a festival of seventeenth- and eighteenth-century music each summer; Cisternino, a small whitewashed hill town; and Ostuni, a truly grand whitewashed town. Egnatia (Egnazia in Italian, from the Greek Gnathia), is a vast archaeological site with a museum displaying examples of delicate black Gnathian ware.

In the Salentine peninsula is Lecce, where sixteenth- and seventeenth-century literary academies earned it the nickname 'The Athens of Apulia' and its architecture from the same period inspired the epithet 'The Florence of the Baroque'. The soft and golden local tufa sandstone is easily carved and was handled with such vigour that it gave rise to an indigenous style called *Barocco leccese*, a religious and secular architecture known more for its lavish decorative elements than its formal innovation. Some of the buildings where it may be seen at its finest include the cathedral, the churches of Santa Croce, Rosario, and Santi Nicola e Cataldo, and the Palazzo Vescovile and Palazzo del Governo, as well as the Convento di Sant'Antonio.

The Greek influence in Apulia becomes most apparent toward the end of the peninsula in such towns as Otranto and Gallipoli. The impact of ancient Greece is even more in evidence at Taranto, a

busy industrial city. Its Museo Nazionale houses collections of sculpture, jewellery, and pottery that distinguish it as the world's most important museum devoted to Magna Graecia, or 'greater Greece'— Greek colonies in present-day Italy.

Calabria, the 'toe' of the Italian boot, shares the same complicated history as the other regions in the area. It preserves an ethnic diversity long since vanished from other parts of Italy which, in addition to the venerable architecture and the natural alpine beauty of the area, make it an attractive destination.

The ethnic mix is first encountered in Guardia Piemontese, a town founded by Waldensian refugees who still speak in Provençal dialect and dress in distinctive folk costumes. Nearby is Paola, the birthplace of Saint Francis of Paola, where an important Minim monastic complex attracts religious pilgrims. Cosenza is Calabria's most culturally lively city, home to the Teatro Rendano, where operas, concerts, and theatre are performed; the Accademia Cosentina, a literary academy that has been active for centuries; and Italy's newest university. Its medieval quarter contains the church of San Domenico, with its beautiful rose window, as well as the cathedral, a Norman castle, and the Museo Civico.

South in Calabria is the city of Reggio di Calabria. Though it was once the ancient Greek colony of Rhegion, virtually nothing remains of its glorious past following numerous sackings, earthquakes, and heavy bombing during World War II. It does, however, boast an excellent museum, the Museo Nazionale della Magna Grecia, of which the undisputed highlights are two larger-than-life bronze statues of warriors found underwater in 1972. Rounding the bend of the toe of Italy are such

Positano is a favourite resort, where the characteristic square white houses and luxuriant gardens descend in steep steps to the sea. In addition to its flower laden hotels and villas, Positano has a tiny harbour, a cathedral, and lots of boutiques.

interesting sights as excavations from the ancient Greek colony of Locri Epizephyrii, complete with its own museum; Gerace, a medieval town dramatically perched on a small mountain plateau overlooking the surrounding plain; the tiny Byzantine church of La Cattolica; and the town of Taverna, birthplace of Calabria's most famous painter, Mattia Preti, whose works may be seen in the churches of San Domenico, Santa Barbara, and San Martino. From there it is a short distance to Catanzaro, the regional capital of Calabria, known for its Museo Provinciale (a museum with a *Madonna and Child* signed by Antonello da Massina) as well as a local dish, *murseddu*, veal and pork innards seasoned with a peppery tomato sauce. Other sights en route include Capo Colonna, where a single column remains of a Doric temple that once had forty-eight, and Rossano, another spectacular Byzantine town. Its Museo Diocesano houses Byzantine masterpiece, the *Codex Purpureus*, an extremely rare illuminated manuscript. North of Rossano, in the neighbouring region of Basilicata, are the extensive excavations of the former Greek colony of Metapontum. Its Antiquarium provides extensive documentation of the excavation, as well as an impressive collection of coins, vases, and statuary unearthed at the site.

Peristyle in the House of the Faun in the excavations at Pompeii. Belonging to the Casii, the house occupied a whole insula, or 'block'. The bronze fauna and much of pavements are on display in Naples.

A perfectly preserved painting depicting The Birth of Venus *from a sumptuous Pompeiian villa. The Pompeiians spared no expense in decorating their villas with such paintings, as well as lavish furniture and objects.*

One of the main streets of Pompeii, excavated and restored. The antiquarian excavations of the site did not begin until as recently as 1748, although some ruins were discovered when an aqueduct was built between 1594 and 1600.

Sicily and Sardinia

*C*omprising the two largest islands in the Mediterranean, Sicily and Sardinia are worth the sea voyage. Both offer remarkable contrasts and a taste of antiquity.

Sicily: A World Apart

The largest island in the Mediterranean, Sicily is a world of its own, a world apart from the rest of Italy. When Sicilians speak of making the twenty-minute crossing from Messina to the mainland, they say they are 'going to Italy', away from the magic and self-contained world as depicted in Tomasi di Lampedusa's *The Leopard*, or the incomprehensibly brutal world of the Mafia as re-created in such films as *The Godfather*. Yet Sicily remains indelibly Italian: 'Sicily is the schoolroom model of Italy for beginners', wrote Luigi Barzini in *The Italians*, 'with every Italian defect magnified, exasperated and brightly coloured'. Sicily retains a powerful hold on the Sicilians. Novelist Leonard Sciascia writes, 'They love their island, but they constantly escape or dream of escaping from it. And when they are away from it, they love it even more and dream of returning'. Perhaps the visitor, too, can understand the strange power of Sicily.

Romantic ruins outside of Agrigento are made even more enchanting by their setting amongst wildflowers and sturdy trees, creating a gentle landscape that has lasted for over two millennia.

The northern coastline of Sicily provides one lovely vista after another of crystal-clear waters and wild terrain. Pristine beaches are set off by a rocky landscape where wildflowers and other lush vegetation abound.

Following page: Agriculture still plays a large part in Sicilian life. Here, a farmer accompanies a rustic horse-drawn cart through parched fields beneath a brilliant blue sky.

Palermo boasts a unique blend of Arab and Norman buildings, such as in the Cappella Palatina in the Palazzo dei Normanni, a fusion of the best of Latin, Byzantine, and Islamic architecture. Near the palace is the Church of San Giovanni degli Eremiti, bursting with red domes on the outside and equally fascinating inside, with its courtyard and cloisters of tropical plants. The cathedral bears the imprint of practically all of Sicily's rulers, the most interesting perhaps being the Norman area in the rear. Nearby are the Quattro Canti, an intersection laid out in the seventeenth century; the church of San Giuseppe dei Tsteatini; the church of the Gesù; and the Archbishop's Palace with the Diocesan Museum.

The Porta Nuova leads to the Convento dei Cappucini, where mummies or skeletons of ecclesiastics or well-to-do citizens are laid out in the clothes they wore in life. Other important churches include La Mortorana, with fine Byzantine mosaics; the church of San Domenico, which can accommodate a congregation of eight thousand; and the Oratorio della Compagnia del Rosario di San Domenico, where the high altar is graced by *The Madonna del Rosario* by Van Dyck.

Palermo also has one of the largest theatres in Italy, Teatro Massimo, which seats 3,200. Other important monuments are the Galleria Nazionale, with its collection of Sicilian painting from the Middle Ages through modern times; the Museo Archeologico, one of Italy's finest archaeological museums; the Galleria Regionale della Sicilia, where Antonello da Messina's *Annunciata* is displayed; and the charming Museo delle Marionette, specialising in Sicilian puppets. Near Palermo are Monreale and Cefalu, which each have Norman cathedrals; Cefalu also has a beach resort.

Between Palermo and Trapani is Segesta, with its evocative ruins of a Doric temple and amphitheatre. Trapani has the Museo Pepoli, displaying paintings as well as

Rulers from many lands left their mark on Sicilian architecture, resulting in unusual combinations of Arab, Norman, and other elements that give the island's architecture its truly unique character.

coral work, a local specialty; its church of Santa Maria del Gesù contains a Della Robbia *Madonna*. Marsala, famous for its wine, has a cathedral with a number of statues by Gagni, the Museo degli Arazzi tapestry museum, and an impressive archaeological museum. At nearby Lilybaeum is a third-century BC Roman villa. Selunite has extensive Greek ruins. Agrigento is the location of the so-called Valley of the Temples—the Temple of Heracles, the Temple of Concord, the Temple of Hera Lacinia, the Temple of Olympian Zeus, and the Temple of Castor and Pollix. Here also is the Norman Church of San Biagi, in which the temple of Demeter is incorporated. Its Museo Archeologico also has an extensive collection of antiquities. Nearby in the section of Agrigento called Caos is the Casa di Pirandello and a museum by the tree where the playwright's ashes are buried.

Further travels will take the inquisitive visitor to Syracuse, one of the most fascinating places in Sicily. Its Old Town lies on the island of Ortygia. Among its monuments are a Temple of Apollo, a cathedral built on the site of a temple of Athena, the Museo Archeologico Nazionale archaeological museum, the Fountain of Arethusa, the Acquario Tropicale (a tropical aquarium), the Palazzo Bellomo, and the Castello Maniace. In the New Town are the Foro Siracusano, a Roman amphitheatre, a Greek theatre, and the most extensive catacombs known in the region.

A number of towns in the southeast are notable for their baroque architecture. The most striking is Noto; others are Ragusa, Modica, Scicli, Grammichele, Canicathi Bagni, and Palazzolo Acreide. Catania is the largest baroque town on the way.

After the Greek theatre and splendid views of Taormina, the remaining sights on Sicily have everything to do with nature. Mount Etna is an active volcano, as is Stromboli, in the Lipari islands.

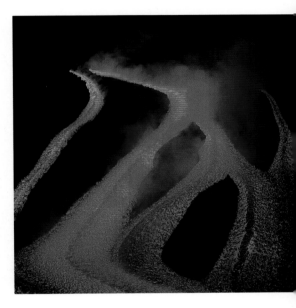

Mount Etna is still quite an active volcano, spewing its rivers of red lava here at night. It doesn't take much imagination to recall the tale of Homer's Cyclops hurling rocks from the side of the volcano at Odysseus.

Sunny Pietraperzia, a lovely Sicilian hill town. Like many of Sicily's hamlets, it is proudly situated high above its surroundings in the midst of luxuriant Mediterranean vegetation.

Dramatically lit against the night sky, this Doric temple at Agrigento is one of the marvels of the Valley of the Temples. All of the valley is especially breathtaking in the evening, when the entire route of temples is floodlit.

The lonely ruins of Segesta evoke the romantic spirit. Here, a Doric temple sits on a flower-dotted hillside, the classical ideal of order amid wild nature. Never finished, the columns were left smooth and the cella, or 'shrine', inside never built.

The fertile fields of Sicily have long earned the island the epithet, 'the granary of Italy', as seen in this field northwest of Agrigento.

Sardinia: The Ancient Isle

The second largest island in the Mediterranean, Sardinia often conjures images of the luxury resorts of the Aga Khan, a very contemporary and chic phenomenon. But the island has been settled since prehistoric times, as evidenced by the massive stone structures called *nuraghi* built between 1500 and 500 BC. Due to the rugged-ness and remoteness of much of the island, Sardinia has preserved many of its old customs and traditions.

Or perhaps it is due to something more, a fierce independence. As Peter Nichols wrote in *Italia, Italia*, 'To be in central Sardinia is to live among people who have rejected every element of what is proudly called European civilisation: the Phoenicians were there and the Romans and the Byzantines, and the Genoese and the Spaniards and the Piedmontese and now, the Italians, and it is as though they had never been. They have all been rejected'.

The largest city in Sardinia is Caligari. Fine views of the city and its setting may be had from the Viale Regina Elena and the Bastione San Remy, a magnificent terrace laid out on partially preserved medieval bas-tions. The cathedral, built by the Pisans in 1312, houses a pulpit from the Pisa cathedral, presented to the Sardinians the same year. The Museo Nazionale Archeologico displays a formidable collection of Punic, Greek, and Roman material as well as the largest collection of Sardinian antiquities. Of particular interest are the bronzes found in the nuraghi. Caligari also has a lovely Roman amphitheatre.

Barumini is a well-preserved city dating from about 1700 BC. Its houses, walls, and towers were built of basalt without mortar, so that the stones continue to withstand the ravages of time.

Nuoro has much of interest, including the house of Grazia Deledda, winner of the Nobel Prize in 1926; a folk museum, the Museo della Vita e delle Tradizioni Populari Sarde, with a charming costume collection; and the Civico Museo Speleo-Archeologico, where ceramics and bronzes found in nearby caves are exhibited.

Alghero, founded in the eleventh century by settlers from Genoa, today survives as a stronghold of Catalan, with street signs written in that language as well as in Italian. Of interest are the fourteenth-century Torre degli Ebrei, built by the Jews before they were expelled by the Inquisition; the fourteenth-century church of San Francesco, a mixture of Gothic arches and Catalan sculpture; and a Renaissance cathedral, where members of the House of Savoy are entombed.

Sassari has a lovely medieval Old City to be explored, with a cathedral dating from the twelfth century. The Museo Sanna is a modern building housing a collection of prehistoric finds to Punic and Roman pieces to folk art. Nature lovers will appreciate the drive along the north coast, replete as it is with spectacular views and fine beaches, a fitting overview of the glories of Italy.

Crystal is one of the most intense colours in Sardinia, as proven by the sky off the southwest coast.

Sardinia's southwest coast is dotted with small sandy beaches with water the colour of turquoise.

INDEX